741.674

# Poster

## Selected from the Graphis Annuals

PAGE ONE PUBLISHING

Cover illustration see p. 132

Works selected from original titles »Graphis Poster«
© 1989, 1990, 1991, 1992, 1993 by
Graphis Press Corp., Dufourstr. 107, CH - 8008 Zürich

© 1994 for this edition: Page One Publishing Pte Ltd, Singapore
Distributed worldwide by
Könemann Verlagsgesellschaft mbH
Bonner Str. 126, D - 50968 Köln

Designed by Peter Feierabend
Foreword by Herbert Lechner
English translation by Karen Williams
French translation by Sylvie Adam-Kuenen
Typesetting by Zentralsatz Dieter Noe
Printed and bound by Toppan Printing

Printed in Singapore
ISBN 981-00-5716-4

# Foreword

»A poster is a scandal!« Thus Raymond Savignac, the doyen of French poster art, postulated the task of large-format commercial art. And indeed, visual provocation and irritation are necessary elements of effective poster design. A poster has to compete for attention amidst the clamour of the outside world. Unlike the magazine advert, glossy brochure, TV slot or radio commercial, it cannot build up an intimate dialogue with its audience. Today, more than ever, it has to be a high-speed medium. The passer-by has no time to spare; he is in too much of a hurry for details, and wants to digest information – if at all – at a glance. An instant later, he is already distracted by other impressions – for a fundamental characteristic of outdoor advertising is that it is sited in particularly busy locations.

So it is that posters must be eye-catching in the truest sense of the word. They must place an optical exclamation mark; they must be comprehensible at a glance – and must captivate their audience on the spot. They must seize the attention, arouse curiosity, and leave the viewer hungry for more.

The great masters of poster art have been courageously and successfully meeting this challenge for over 100 years, creating an art of the streets that depends on ever new, fascinating motifs. Mercifully, there is no patent recipe for the ideal poster; instead, we find a breath-taking variety of themes, styles and techniques. Whether a photograph or an illustration, whether employing all the colours of the rainbow or in sober black-and-white typography, whether naïve, superrealist or surrealist, whether classical or experimental – every avenue is explored.

Amidst this concert of massed and at times shrill voices, it is remarkable to observe how even quiet and reticent posters make their message heard. Seemingly clear and simple, they nevertheless succeed in catching our eye and lodging in our minds.

As fashions and subjects change, and as new products and advertisers discover the vehicle of the poster, so the two-dimensional world of the billboard continues to expand. Consumer goods and the arts, tourism and social topics, politics and local news – all are expressed in this large-scale format.

The poster, fast and ephemeral, is dead – and is born anew every day. As long as graphic artists, photographers, illustrators and copywriters continue to devote their powers of imagination to reinventing the poster, it need fear neither the competition of electronic media nor the weariness of a supersaturated public.

The proof can be found in the present book, which collects outstanding examples of works by an international selection of modern poster artists.

# Vorwort

»Ein Plakat ist ein Skandal« – so postulierte der Doyen der französischen Plakatkunst, Raymond Savignac, die Aufgabe der Werbekunst im Großformat. Optische Provokation und Irritation des Betrachters sind jedenfalls notwendige Voraussetzungen für einen wirkungsvollen Entwurf. Denn das Plakat muß sich gegen eine vielfältige Konkurrenz im öffentlichen Raum durchsetzen, es kann nicht auf eine gleichsam dialogartige Intimität wie Anzeige, Prospekt, TV- oder Hörfunkspot bauen. Deshalb ist es – mehr denn je – ein schnelles Medium. Der Passant hat keine Zeit, er will – wenn überhaupt! – »auf einen Blick« informiert sein, er hat es zu eilig für Details, wird bereits wieder abgelenkt von anderen Eindrücken – denn ein Wesenszug der Außenwerbung ist ja gerade, daß sie bevorzugt an besonders belebten Stellen plaziert wird.

Plakativ im besten Sinne des Wortes müssen deshalb die Blätter sein, ein optisches Ausrufezeichen, auf einen Blick erfaßbar – und den flüchtigen Betrachter sofort in den Bann schlagend. Die Aufmerksamkeit wecken, Neugierde schaffen, hungrig machen auf mehr.

Seit über 100 Jahren gelingt es den Großmeistern des Plakates dieses Ziel mit ihren Entwürfen bravourös zu erreichen. Und eine Kunst der Straße mit immer neuen, faszinierenden Motiven zu verwirklichen. Schön, daß es kein Patentrezept für das ideale Plakat gibt, denn so entsteht eine atemberaubende Vielfalt aus Themen, Stilen, Techniken. Foto und Illustration, die ganze Skala des Regenbogens und strenge Typographie, Naives, Hyperrealistisches oder Surreales, Klassisches und Experiment – alle Möglichkeiten sind vertreten.

Faszinierend, daß sich in diesem vielstimmigen und bisweilen schrillen Konzert auch jene ganz stillen und zurückhaltenden Plakate Aufmerksamkeit zu verschaffen wissen. Jene scheinbar ganz einfachen und klaren Blätter, auf denen der Blick haften bleibt und die selbst haften bleiben im Gedächtnis.

Die Moden und die Sujets verändern sich, neue Produkte und Absender entdecken das Plakat und bereichern so den zweidimensionalen Zirkus auf der Anschlagfläche noch weiter. Bunte Warenwelt und Kultur, Touristik und soziale Themen, Politik und Lokales, alles findet die adäquate Umsetzung im Großformat.

Das Plakat, ein schnelles Medium und schnell vergänglich, ist tot – und wird jeden Tag neugeboren. Es muß weder die Konkurrenz der elektronischen Medien noch die Ermüdung eines übersättigten Publikums fürchten, solange Grafikdesigner, Fotografen, Illustratoren und Texter ihren ganzen Einfallsreichtum in die immer neue Erfindung des Plakates legen!

Den Beweis bieten die Beispiele des vorliegenden Bandes, in dem die internationalen Spitzenleistungen der modernen Plakatkünstler versammelt sind.

# Préface

«Une affiche est un scandale». Telle est la mission artistique de la publicité grand format que le doyen de l'art de l'affiche en France, Raymond Savignac, érigeait en postulat. La provocation et l'irritation du nerf optique de celui qui regarde sont dans tous les cas la condition sine qua non du succès. Car l'affiche doit s'imposer face à la concurrence multiforme dans l'espace public. Elle n'a pas le caractère en quelque sorte intime de l'annonce, du prospectus, du message publicitaire à la télévision ou à la radio. Elle est donc – plus que jamais – un média rapide. Le passant n'a pas de temps à perdre. Il veut – si tant est qu'il le veuille – être informé en «un clin d'œil». Il est bien trop pressé pour s'arrêter aux détails, et d'autres impressions viennent bientôt distraire son attention. C'est en effet dans la nature même de la publicité extérieure de choisir, de préférence, justement les endroits particulièrement animés.

Elle se doit donc de s'afficher, au meilleur sens du terme, d'être un point d'exclamation que l'œil embrasse en une seconde, et qui capture immédiatement le passant fugitif. D'éveiller l'attention, d'allumer la curiosité, de donner l'envie d'en savoir plus. Depuis plus de cent ans, les grands maîtres de l'affiche y parviennent avec brio. Il leur est donné d'exercer un art de la rue à l'aide de motifs toujours nouveaux et fascinants. Il n'existe pas de méthode éprouvée de l'affiche idéale. Et c'est tant mieux! D'où une multitude stupéfiante de thèmes, de styles et de techniques. La photographie et l'illustration, toute la palette des couleurs de l'arc-en-ciel, la rigueur de la typographie, le naïf, l'hyperréaliste ou le surréaliste, le classique et l'expérimental – toutes les possibilités sont représentées.

Il est fascinant de s'apercevoir que, dans ce concert à plusieurs voix et de temps à autre strident, des affiches calmes et discrètes savent, elles aussi, se faire entendre. Ce sont des feuilles apparemment simples et claires qui capturent le regard et se gravent dans la mémoire.

Les modes et les sujets changent. Des produits et des bailleurs de fonds nouveaux découvrent l'affiche, et viennent ainsi enrichir le spectacle à deux dimensions qui se déploie sur les panneaux d'affichage. Le monde coloré des produits et la culture, le tourisme et les thèmes sociaux, la politique et les affaires locales – le grand format convient à tout.

L'affiche, expéditive aussi bien qu'éphémère, meurt et renaît chaque jour. Elle ne doit redouter ni la concurrence des moyens de communication électroniques ni la lassitude d'un public sursaturé, tant que les stylistes-graphistes, les photographes, les illustrateurs et les rédacteurs publicitaires continueront de mettre toute la force de leur imagination au service de la création de nouvelles affiches.

On en voudra pour preuve les exemples contenus dans le présent album, qui rassemble les hauts faits par lesquels les artistes modernes de l'affiche s'illustrent partout dans le monde.

Art Director
S. & J. Jupin
Designer
S. & J. Jupin
Photographer
S. & J. Jupin
Client
Palais des Congres et de la Culture

Graphic Design Today

グラフィックデザインの今日

東京国立近代美術館 工芸館
1990.9.26. Wed.-11.11.Sun.(Closed on Mondays.)
AM10:00-PM5:00 (Visitors are acceptable until 4:30pm.)
Takebashi Station on the Tozai Subway Line.
Organized by The National Museum of Modern Art, Tokyo.
in Cooperation with Toppan Printing Co.,Ltd.

Makoto Saito

*Art Director*
Makoto Saito
*Designer*
Makoto Saito
*Client*
The National Museum of Modern Art

CEMENT I 100 ÅR
AALBORG HISTORISKE MUSEUM
2. JUNI · 22. OKTOBER

Painting: Brad Holland ©1990  Separation: Scan Graphics  Paper: Field Paper Co.  Printing: Holm Graphics

*Art Director*
Brad Holland
*Designers*
Brad Holland, Jim McCune
*Artist*
Brad Holland
*Client*
Des Moines Art Director Association

*Art Director*
Ole Flyv Christensen
*Designer*
Ole Flyv Christensen
*Agency*
Ole Flyv Christensen
*Client*
Aalborg Portland

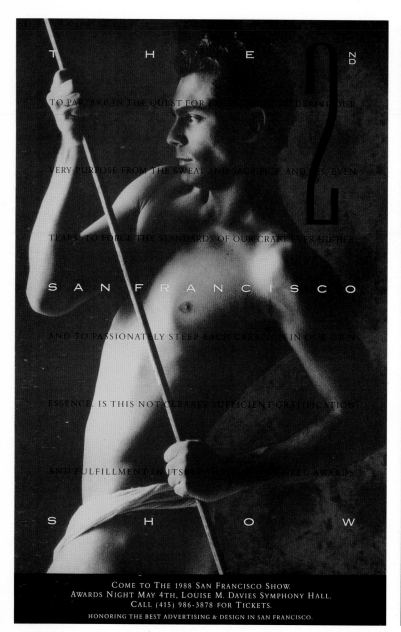

Art Director
Michael Mabry
Designers
Michael Mabry, Piper Murakami
Photographer
Gerald Bybee
Copywriter
Paul Cuneo
Agency
Michael Mabry Design
Client
San Francisco Art Directors Club
and San Francisco Ad Club

Art Directors
Neil Davis, Ira Levy
Designer
Neil Davis
Agency
Neil Davis Design
Client
Vassar College Art Gall

DORA

VIENNA & PARIS
1907 – 1957
THE PHOTOGRAPHY OF DORA KALLMUS

ORGANIZED BY THE
VASSAR COLLEGE ART GALLERY
POUGHKEEPSIE · NEW YORK · APRIL 1 – JUNE 7

AND PARTICIPATING
FASHION INSTITUTE OF TECHNOLOGY
NEW YORK · JUNE 23 – AUGUST 1

THE JOHN & MABLE RINGLING MUSEUM OF ART
SARASOTA · OCTOBER 9 – DECEMBER 27, 1987

Art Director
Pierre Mendell
Agency
Mendell & Oberer
Client
Design Center Stuttgart

Designer
A. R. Penck
Artist
A. R. Penck
Client
Kunsthaus Zürich

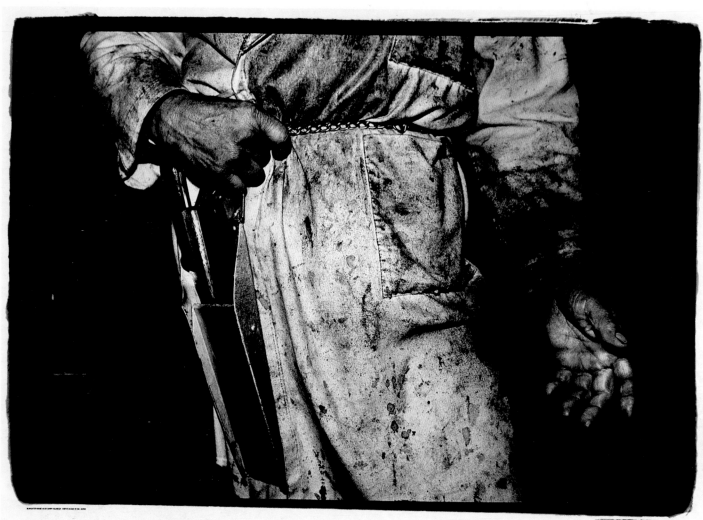

Art Directors
George Lips, Bill Shinn
Designer
Bill Shinn
Photographer
Barry Holniker
Agency
Barton-Gillet
Client
Maryland Art Place, Baltimore

Designer
Werner Jeker
Photographer
Man Ray
Client
Kunsthaus Zürich, Schweiz.
Stiftung für die Photographi

Kunsthaus
Zürich

12. März bis
23. Mai 1988

Öffnungszeiten:
Montag                          14-17 Uhr
Dienstag bis Freitag            10-17 Uhr
Samstag und Sonntag             10-21 Uhr
Ostern
31. März 1988                   10-15 Uhr
Samstag, 1. April 1988          geschlossen
2./3. April 1988                geschlossen
4. April 1988                   10-17 Uhr
Sechseläuten
18. April 1988                  geschlossen
1. Mai 1988
11. Mai 1988                    10-15 Uhr
12. Mai 1988                    10-17 Uhr
Pfingsten
Sonntag, 22. Mai 1988           geschlossen
23. Mai 1988                    10-17 Uhr

Schweizerische
Stiftung für
die Photographie

Photographien
Filme
Frühe Objekte

M    A          N

R    A          Y

Man Ray: Femme aux longs cheveux, 1929  Design: Werner Jeker  Serigraphie: Albin Uldry

*Art Director*
Mirko Ilic
*Designer*
Nicky Lindeman
*Artist*
Mirko Ilic
*Client*
Yugoslav Cultural Center,
New York

t Director
th Humerind
esigner
th Humerind
otographer
t Veermäe
ient
OREK

Art Director
Masami Shimizu
Designer
Masami Shimizu
Photographer
Yoshihiko Ueda
Client
Takeo Co., Ltd.

# FOTOS FÜR MILLIONEN

Eine Ausstellung der
Josef-Haubrich-Kunsthalle in Zusammenarbeit
mit dem Kölnischen Kunstverein.
Vom 3. Oktober bis 6. November 1988.

7 Bilderschauen
im Rahmen des Kodak Kulturprogramms:

ODYSSEE – Die schönsten Fotos aus National Geographic
40 JAHRE ZEITGESCHEHEN – 40 Jahre STERN
DIE ZEIT IM BILD – Fotojournalismus in Amerika
DIE KUNST, MIT BILDERN ZU ÜBERZEUGEN – Eine Geschichte der Werbefotografie
YOU PRESS THE BUTTON – WE DO THE REST. Aus den Kindertagen der Schnappschußfotografie
AUGENZEUGEN – World Press Photo 1988
DIE WAHRHEIT BEKENNT FARBE – Contact Press Images

Täglich von 10 bis 17 Uhr, Di. und Fr. bis 20 Uhr.
Verlängerte Öffnungszeiten
während der photokina (4. + 6. bis 11. 10.):
täglich 10 bis 20 Uhr.

Stadt Köln

OUVERTURE DE LA GALERIE JUNKO KOSHINO
JEUDI LE 16 NOVEMBRE, 1989

La GALERIE JUNKO KOSHINO vous invite à sa salle Espace Futur où vous retrouverez une exposition de Mode et de Laques ainsi que sa Boutique qui met en valeur un concept global du design pour notre vie et l'environnement.

JUNKO KOSHINO
10 AV. MONTAIGNE PARIS

*Art Director*
Katsuhiro Kinoshita
*Designer*
Katsuhiro Kinoshita
*Photographer*
Shigeyuki Morishita
*Agency*
Design Club, Inc.
*Client*
Junko Koshino Design Office Ltd.

◁ *Art Director*
Hans-Georg Pospischil
*Designer*
Bernadette Gotthardt
*Artist*
Alfons Holtgreve
*Client*
Kodak Kulturprogramm,
Josef-Haubrich-Kunsthalle, Köln

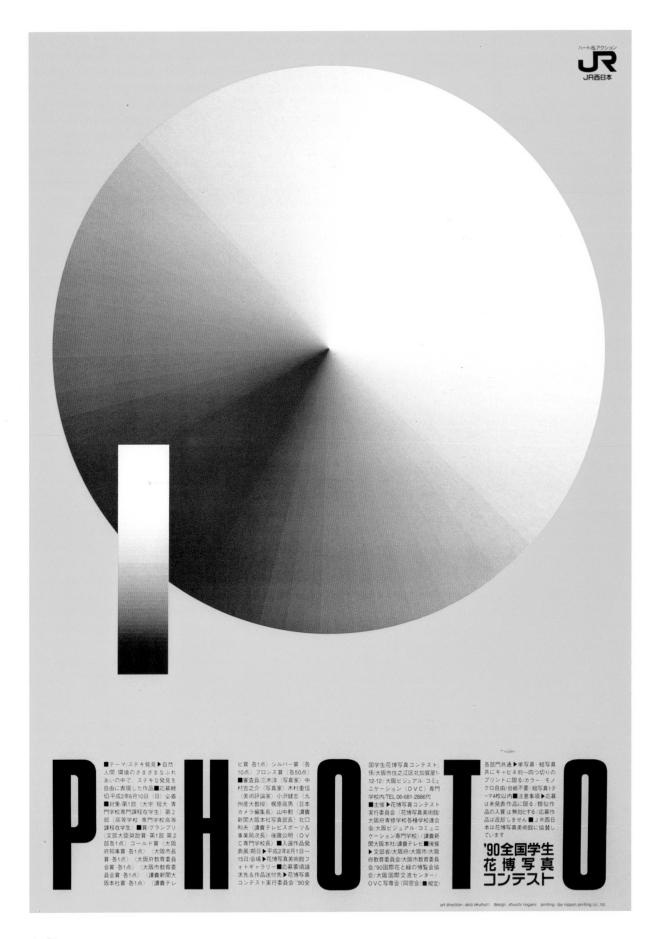

*Art Director*
Akio Okumura
*Designer*
Shuichi Nogami
*Agency*
Packaging Create Inc.
*Client*
Flower Expo

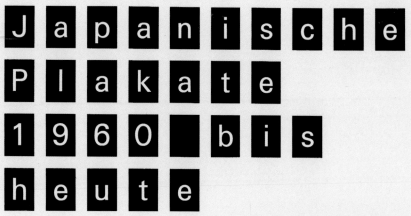

Japanische
Plakate
1960 bis
heute

26. Oktober 1988
bis 15. Januar 1989
Dienstag bis Sonntag
10 bis 17 Uhr
Die Neue Sammlung
Prinzregentenstrasse 3
München

YAGAMI KAZUTOSHI SILK SCREEN
EXHIBITION
October 31 monday 1987→September 5 suturday 1987
11:00a.m.→7:00p.m.
GALLERY SHIROTA
7-10-8 Ginza Chuo-ku Tokyo Telephone 03-572-7971
八神和敏版画展
1987年8月31日㊊→9月5日㊏
シロタ画廊
東京都中央区銀座7-10-8

*Art Director*
Kazutoshi Yagami
*Designer*
Kazutoshi Yagami
*Photographer*
Kazutoshi Yagami
*Client*
Gallery Shirota

*Art Director*
Pierre Mendell
*Designer*
Pierre Mendell
*Photographer*
Klaus Oberer
*Agency*
Mendell & Oberer
*Client*
Die Neue Sammlung, München

*Art Director*
Gottfried Helnwein
*Designer*
Gottfried Helnwein
*Photographer*
Gottfried Helnwein
*Client*
Kulturzentrum Mainz

*Art Director*
Roger Pfund
*Designer*
Roger Pfund
*Copywriter*
Roger Pfund
*Agency*
Atelier Roger Pfund
*Client*
Musée International de
la Croix-Rouge, Genève

17 Avenue de la Paix
1202 Genève
Tél 022 33 26 60

à proximité du
Palais des Nations

Ouverture
tous les jours
de 10 à 17 h
sauf le mardi

Musée International
de la Croix-Rouge

Histoire du mouvement
de la Croix-Rouge
et du Croissant-Rouge

Internationales Museum
des Roten Kreuzes

Geschichte der Bewegung
des Roten Kreuzes
und des Roten Halbmondes

International Museum
of the Red Cross

History
of the Red Cross and
Red Crescent movement

17 Avenue de la Paix
1202 Genève

à proximité du
Palais des Nations

Ouverture
tous les jours
de 10 à 17 h
sauf le mardi

*Art Director*
Peter Pocs
*Designer*
Peter Pocs
*Photographer*
Laszlo Haris
*Client*
Mairie de Castelmoron

*Art Director*
Jenö Gerendy
*Designer*
Jenö Gerendy
*Client*
Obuda Galeria

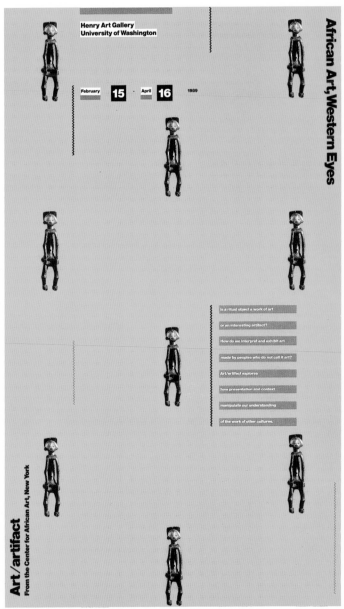

Art Director
Shigeo Fukuda
Designer
Shigeo Fukuda
Artist
Shigeo Fukuda
Client
The Yomiuri Shimbun

Art Director
Douglas Wadden
Designer
Douglas Wadden
Agency
Design Collaborative/Seattle
Client
Henry Art Gallery/
University of Washington

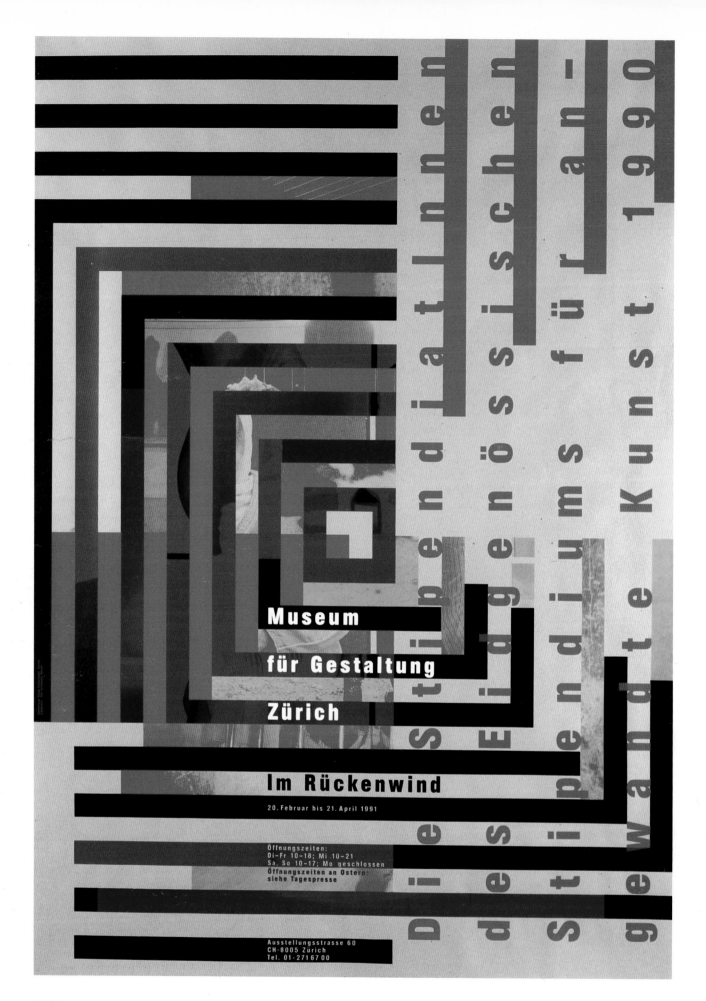

Art Director
Ralph Schraivogel
*Designer*
Ralph Schraivogel
*Client*
Museum für Gestaltung, Zürich

SOLOMON R. GUGGENHEIM MUSEUM, NEW YORK. PHOTO: ROBERT E. MATES.

FRANK LLOYD WRIGHT

IN THE REALM OF IDEAS

Art Path provides curriculum specific tours for Dade County Public School students.

The Art Path project is a coalition of Dade County's Center for the Fine Arts; Board of County Commissioners, Metropolitan Dade County; and the Dade County Public Schools. Art Path is a program originated by the Junior League of Miami, Inc.

The exhibition and its tour have been made possible by the generous support of Kohler Co. and Whirlpool Corporation. The City of Scottsdale has provided funding for the construction of the Usonian Automatic Exhibition House. Organized and circulated by the Scottsdale Cultural Council and The Frank Lloyd Wright Foundation. Local funding has been provided by a generous grant from Burdines.

"ARCHITECTURE IS THE TRIUMPH OF HUMAN IMAGINATION OVER MATERIALS, METHODS AND MEN, TO PUT MAN INTO POSSESSION OF HIS OWN EARTH."

 Southern Bell
A BELLSOUTH Company

THIS EDUCATIONAL POSTER HAS BEEN MADE POSSIBLE BY THE GENEROSITY OF SOUTHERN BELL, A BELLSOUTH COMPANY.

DECEMBER 18, 1988 - FEBRUARY 26, 1989

© CENTER FOR THE FINE ARTS, ART PATH, 1988

ABOVE QUOTATIONS FROM FRANK LLOYD WRIGHT.
© THE FRANK LLOYD WRIGHT FOUNDATION, 1988

*Art Director*
Jacques Auger
*Designer*
Patrick J. Hamilton
*Agency*
Jacques Auger Design Associates
*Client*
Center for the Fine Arts, Miami

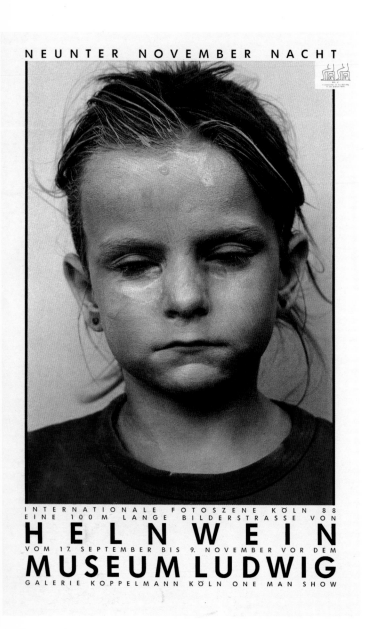

Art Director
Gottfried Helnwein
Designer
Gottfried Helnwein
Artist
Gottfried Helnwein
Client
Museum Ludwig, Köln

Art Director
Ulrike Budde
Designer
Uwe Göbel
Client
Haus der Kunst, München

Dante Saganías, pinturas recientes. 30 de marzo al 16 de abril.
Galería Lagard, Suipacha 1216, Buenos Aires. Tel. 393 7822.
Lunes a viernes de 11 a 20 horas y sábados de 10.30 a 13 horas.

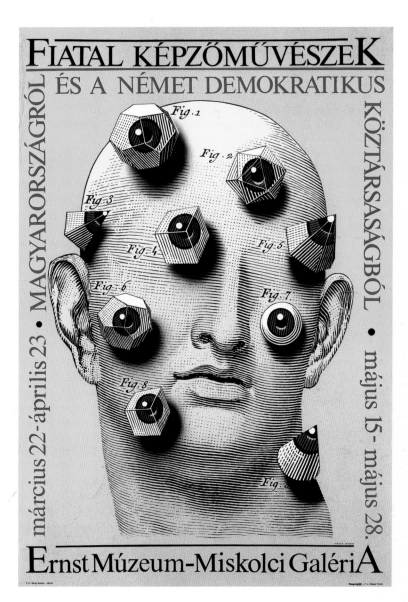

*Designer*
Gustavo Pedroza
*Illustrator*
Gustavo Pedroza
*Agency*
Gustavo Pedroza
*Client*
Dante Saganias

*Art Director*
Hedi Szepes
*Designer*
Istvan Orosz
*Artist*
Istvan Orosz
*Copywriter*
Istvan Orosz
*Client*
Mücsarnok/Katalin Neray

*Designer*
Claude Kuhn
*Client*
Naturhistorisches Museum
der Bürgergemeinde Bern

*Art Director*
Niklaus Troxler
*Designer*
Niklaus Troxler
*Illustrator*
Niklaus Troxler
*Agency*
Niklaus Troxler Grafik-Studio
*Client*
Kulturamt Stadt Luzern

Designer
Taku Tashiro
*Illustrator*
Taku Tashiro
*Client*
Tokyo Illustrators Society

▷ *Designer*
Milton Glaser
*Illustrator*
Milton Glaser
*Client*
Philadelphia Zoo

▷▷ *Art Director*
Andreas Karl
*Designer*
Andreas Karl
*Illustrator*
Andreas Karl
*Copywriter*
Andreas Karl
*Stylist*
Andreas Karl
*Agency*
Kienow + Partner
*Client*
Ministerium für Bildung + Kultur
Rheinland-Pfalz

The Philadelphia Zoo
CARNIVORE KINGDOM
Milton Glaser
Sponsored by
Bell of Pennsylvania
in support of the Philadelphia Zoo's new carnivore exhibit. Poster sales will also be used to support this endeavor.

# KULTURSOMMER '92

**SOMMERTHEATER
KLOSTERRUINE LIMBURG**
Bad Dürkheim

**INTERNATIONALES
JAZZFESTIVAL**
Kammgarn Kaiserslautern

**ZAUBERFLÖTE PUR**
Chawwerusch-Theater unterwegs

**BALLETT DER WELT**
Theater im Pfalzbau, Ludwigshafen

**SCHLOSSTAGE
PANTOMIME-FESTIVAL**
Idar-Oberstein

**MOSELFESTWOCHEN**

**'OPEN WALD'**
Natur und Kultur

**TAL-TOTAL**
Der Erlebnistag
im Tal der Loreley

**VILLA MUSICA**
in Burgen und Schlössern

**THEATERTAGE**
in der Landskrone Oppenheim

**DOROTHY PARKER**
Szenen und Chansons,
Kammerspiele Mainz

**KULTURBEUTEL**

**LANDESJUGEND-
BLASORCHESTER**

**INTERNATIONALES
THEATERFESTIVAL HAMBACH**

**AHNUNG DER STILLE**
Tanztheater Regenbogen unterwegs

**STAATSTHEATER MAINZ
„CONTACT '92"**
Tage des polnischen Theaters

**FEMME CULTURELLE**
Mainz

**'BURGENZAUBER'**
Theater für Kinder aus Europa

**EURO-T(R)ANS '92**
Trans-Europe Halles- und
Internationales Tanztheaterfestival,
Kulturfabrik Koblenz

**'VER-RÜCKTE GRENZEN'**
Rocktheater-Revue in und um Trier

**RHEINISCHE PHILHARMONIE**

**FIDELIO OPEN-AIR
EHRENBREITSTEIN**
Theater der Stadt Koblenz

**KINDER- UND
JUGENDTHEATERFESTIVAL**
Speyer

**INTERNATIONALES
AMATEUR BIG BAND-FESTIVAL**
Koblenz

**LANDESJUGENDCHOR**

**KUZ-SOMMER**
Mainz

**LAHNECK LIVE**
Lahnstein

**INTERNATIONALE
ORGELFESTWOCHEN**

**KULTUR FÜR KURZE**
Montabaur

**JUGENDNACHWUCHSFESTIVAL**
Rock & Pop am Deutschen Eck,
Koblenz

**OPEN OHR FESTIVAL**
Mainz

**GAUKLERFESTIVAL**
Koblenz

**JAZZ UND KUNST
IN WEINGÜTERN**

**STAATSPHILHARMONIE
RHEINLAND-PFALZ**

**JACQUES OFFENBACH-
FESTIVAL** Bad Ems

**MUSIK MIT
PFEFFERMINZGESCHMACK**
Schloßtreff Deidesheim

**DEUTSCHES MOZARTFEST
ZWEIBRÜCKEN**
Oper im Zirkus

**FEST DER NATIONEN**
Trier

**JAZZ-ORCHESTER
RHEINLAND-PFALZ**

**FESTIVAL DER FANTASIE**
Jockgrim

**BURGFESTSPIELE MAYEN**

Eine Initiative des Landes Rheinland-Pfalz

Sie erhalten:
Infos und Kultursommer-Programmheft
bei allen Veranstaltern, beim Büro Kultursommer
im Ministerium für Bildung und Kultur,
Postfach 3220, 6500 Mainz und unter 01 30/82 55 82
Aktuelle Programmhinweise: Im Südwesttext auf Videotext-Tafel 505

# RHEINLAND-PFALZ

◁◁ *Art Director*
Jennifer Morla
*Illustrator*
Jennifer Morla
*Agency*
Morla Design
*Client*
Stanford Alumni Association

◁ *Art Director*
Efim Zwik
*Designer*
Efim Zwik
*Artist*
Efim Zwik

*Art Director*
Craig Frazier
*Designer*
Craig Frazier
*Artist*
Craig Frazier
*Agency*
Frazier Design
*Client*
Western Merchandise Mart,
San Francisco

*Art Director*
Volker Müller
*Designer*
Volker Müller
*Agency*
V. Müller/R. Bauer
*Client*
Öffentliche Bibliotheken,
Baden-Württemberg

BIBLIOTHEKEN BADEN-WÜRTTEMBERG

VIERTE WOCHE DER

5. - 13. MAI 1990

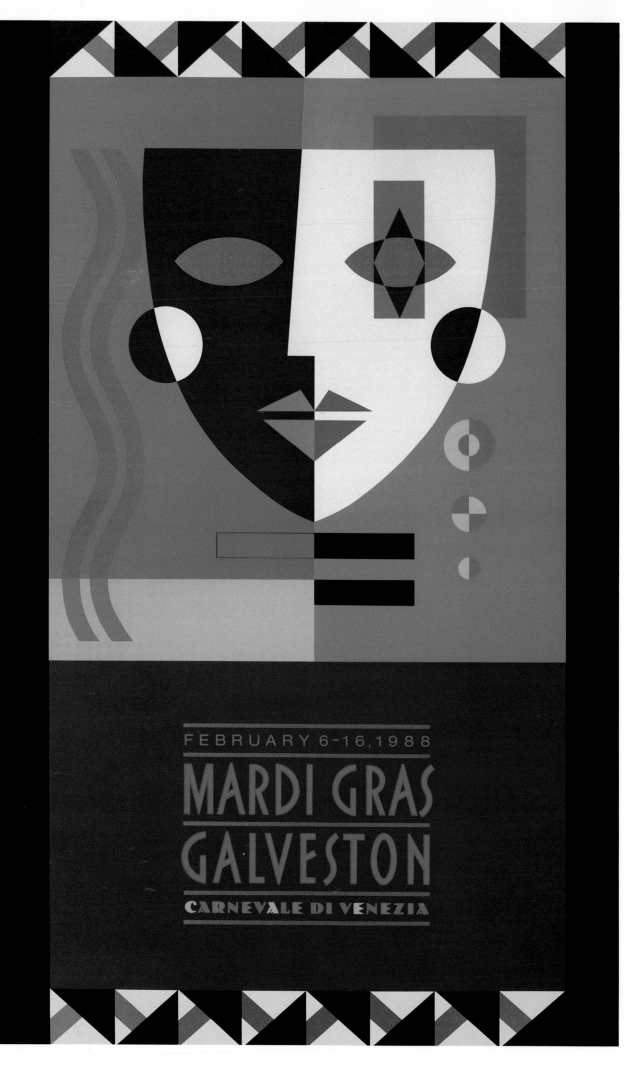

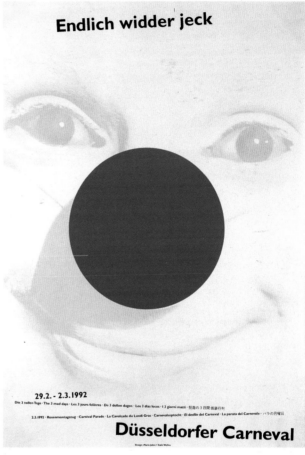

*Art Director*
Jahns + Wallau
*Designer*
Jahns + Wallau
*Client*
Stadt Düsseldorf

*Art Director*
Don Sibley
*Designer*
Don Sibley
*Artist*
Don Sibley
*Agency*
Dancie P. Ware
*Studio*
Sibley/Peteet Design
*Client*
Galveston Park Board
of Trustees

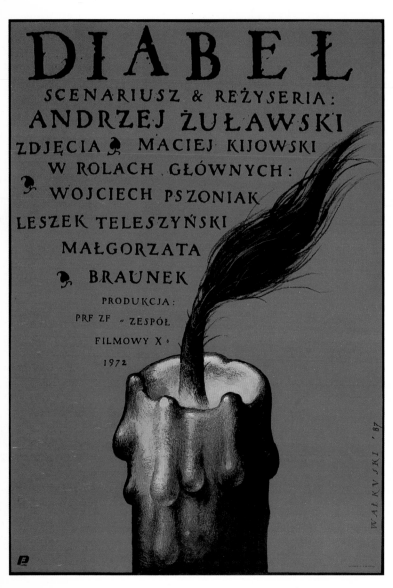

Artist
Wieslaw Walkuski
Client
Polfilm

Art Director
Egon Bavcer
Designer
Egon Bavcer
Artist
Franci Virant
Client
Slovene National Theatre,
Maribor

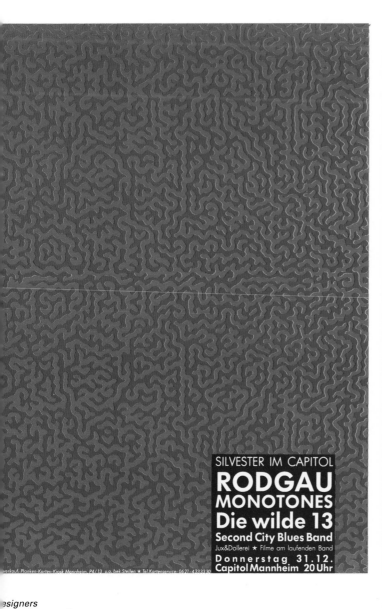

Designers
rhard Fontagnier,
bine Kranz
gency
uchladen
ient
xtra-Veranstaltungen GmbH

Designer
Christer Themptander
Artist
Christer Themptander
Client
Kulturhuset Stockholm

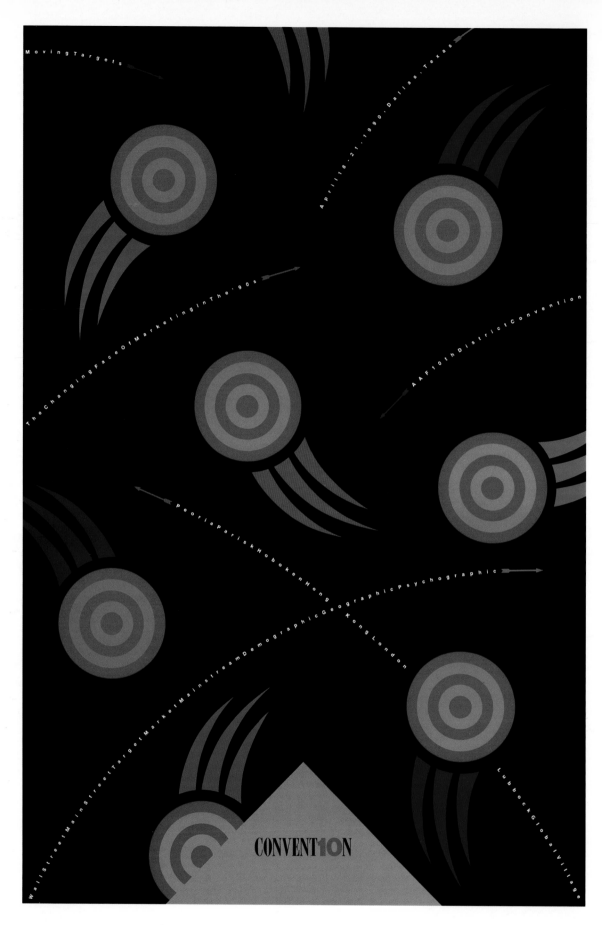

Art Director
John Swieter
Designers
Paul Munsterman,
John Swieter, Jim Vogel
Copywriter
Katherine Holland
Agency
Swieter Design
Client
American Advertising
Federation

Art Director
Vanderbyl Design
Designer
Vanderbyl Design
Illustrator
Vanderbyl Design
Agency
Vanderbyl Design
Client
Exhibitor Magazine

*Designer*
Andreas Wallat
*Artist*
Andreas Wallat
*Client*
ICOGRADA-Komitee
der DDR

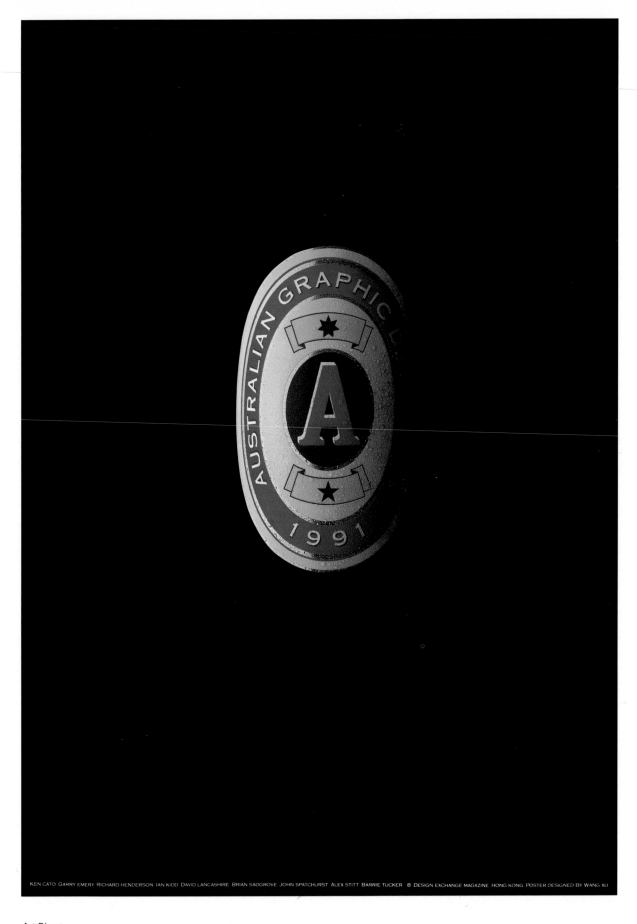

KEN CATO GARRY EMERY RICHARD HENDERSON IAN KIDD DAVID LANCASHIRE BRIAN SADGROVE JOHN SPATCHURST ALEX STITT BARRIE TUCKER 8 DESIGN EXCHANGE MAGAZINE HONG KONG POSTER DESIGNED BY WANG XU

*Art Director*
Wang Xu
*Designer*
Wang Xu
*Photographer*
Ka-Sing Lee
*Agency*
Editorial Office of *Design Exchange*
*Publisher*
*Design Exchange* Magazine

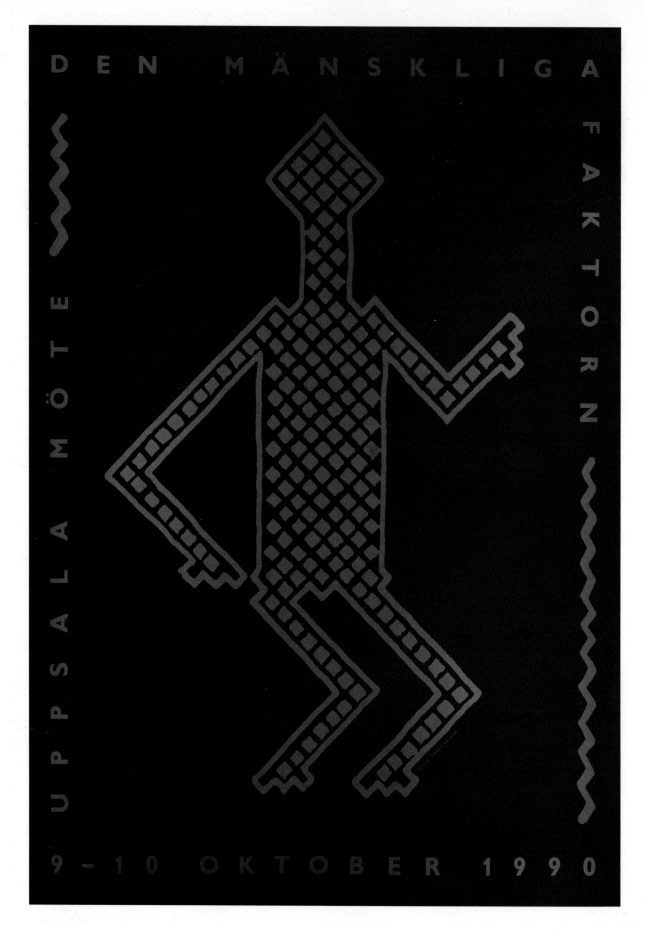

Art Director
Gabor Palotai
Designer
Gabor Palotai
Illustrator
Gabor Palotai
Agency
Gabor Palotai Design
Client
Uppsala University

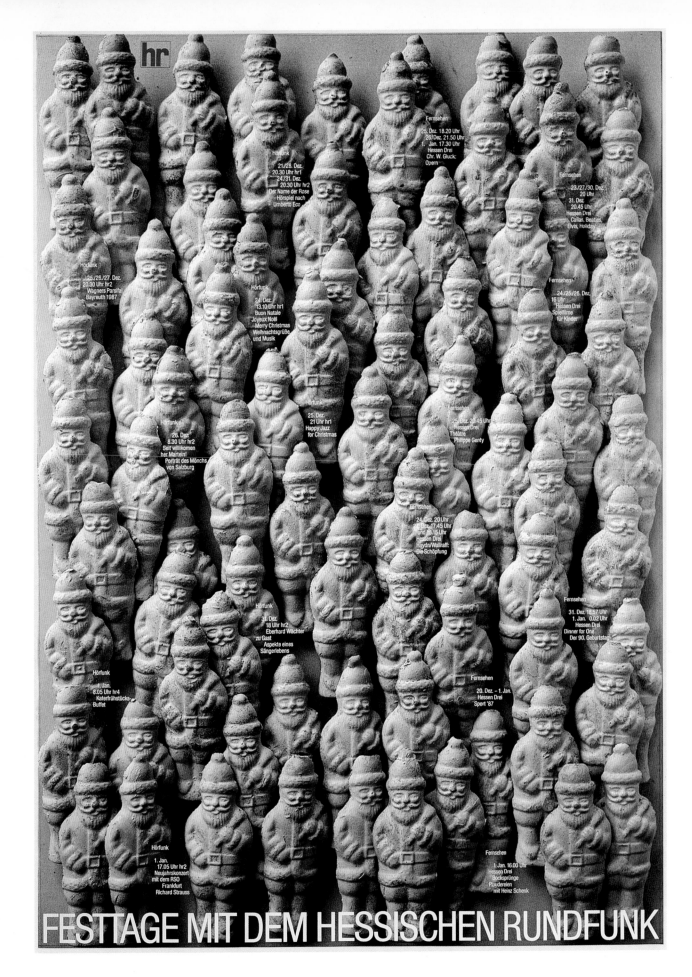

**FESTTAGE MIT DEM HESSISCHEN RUNDFUNK**

*Art Director*
Günther Kieser
*Designer*
Günther Kieser
*Agency*
Hessischer Rundfunk/
Abt. Publizistik
*Client*
Hessischer Rundfunk

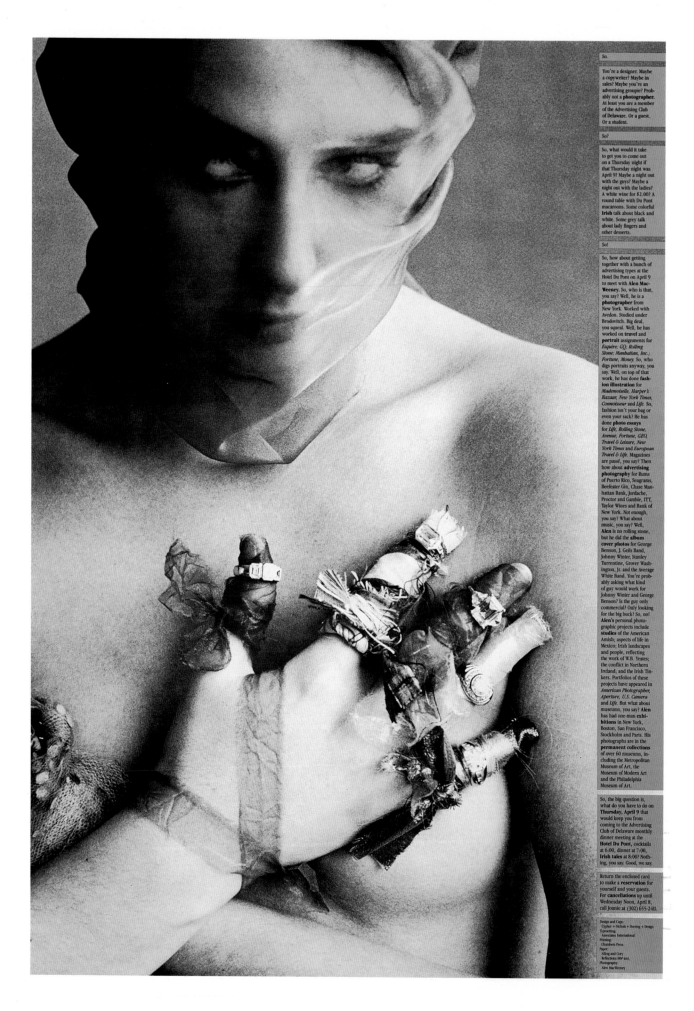

You're a designer. Maybe a copywriter? Maybe in sales? Maybe you're an advertising groupie? Probably not a **photographer.** At least you are a member of the Advertising Club of Delaware. Or a guest. Or a student.

**So?**

So, what would it take to get you to come out on a Thursday night if that Thursday night was April 9? Maybe a night out with the guys? Maybe a night out with the ladies? A white wine for $2.00? A round table with Du Pont macaroons. Some colorful **Irish** talk about black and white. Some grey talk about lady fingers and other desserts.

**So!**

So, how about getting together with a bunch of advertising types at the Hotel Du Pont on April 9 to meet with **Alen Mac-Weeney.** So, who is that, you say? Well, he is a **photographer** from New York. Worked with Avedon. Studied under Brodovitch. Big deal, you squeal. Well, he has worked on travel and **portrait** assignments for *Esquire; GQ; Rolling Stone; Manhattan, Inc.; Fortune, Money.* So, who digs portraits anyway, you say. Well, on top of that work, he has done **fashion illustration** for *Mademoiselle, Harper's Bazaar, New York Times, Connoisseur* and *Life.* So, fashion isn't your bag or even your sack? He has done **photo essays** for *Life, Rolling Stone, Avenue, Fortune, GEO, Travel & Leisure, New York Times* and *European Travel & Life.* Magazines are passé, you say? Then how about **advertising photography** for Rums of Puerto Rico, Seagrams, Beefeater Gin, Chase Manhattan Bank, Jordache, Proctor and Gamble, ITT, Taylor Wines and Bank of New York. Not enough, you say? What about music, you say? Well, **Alen** is no rolling stone, but he did the **album cover photos** for George Benson, J. Geils Band, Johnny Winter, Stanley Turrentine, Grover Washington, Jr. and the Average White Band. You're probably asking what kind of guy would work for Johnny Winter and George Benson? Is the guy only commercial? Only looking for the big buck? So, no! **Alen's** personal photographic projects include **studies** of the American Amish; aspects of life in Mexico; Irish landscapes and people, reflecting the work of W.B. Yeates; the conflict in Northern Ireland; and the Irish Tinkers. Portfolios of these projects have appeared in *American Photographer, Aperture, U.S. Camera* and *Life.* But what about museums, you say? **Alen** has had one-man exhibitions in New York, Boston, San Francisco, Stockholm and Paris. His photographs are in the **permanent collections** of over 60 museums, including the Metropolitan Museum of Art, the Museum of Modern Art and the Philadelphia Museum of Art.

So, the big question is, what do you have to do on **Thursday, April 9** that would keep you from coming to the Advertising Club of Delaware monthly dinner meeting at the **Hotel Du Pont,** cocktails at 6:00, dinner at 7:00, **Irish tales** at 8:00? Nothing, you say. Good, we say.

Return the enclosed card to make a **reservation** for yourself and your guests. For **cancellations** up until Wednesday Noon, April 8, call Joanie at (302) 655-2411.

Design and Copy:
Cypher + Nicholl + Deering + Design
Typesetting:
Associates International
Printing:
Chambers Press
Paper:
Alling and Grey
Reflections 80# text.
Photography:
Alen MacWeeney.

TO THE
PEOPLE OF
CINCINNATI

designer: Anne Ghory-Goodman / photographer: Anne Ghory-Goodman / assistants: Patricia Alterneau, Katherine Johnson / typesetter: Pagemakers / printer: Berman Printing Company / color separator: R.P.I. Color Service, Inc. / paper: Johnston Paper Company

*Art Directors*
Ray Nichols, Jill Cypher
*Designers*
Ray Nichols, Jill Cypher
*Photographer*
Alen MacWeeney
*Copywriter*
Ray Nichols
*Agency*
Cypher + Nichols + Design
*Client*
Advertising Club
of Delaware

◁ *Art Director*
Anne Ghory-Goodman
*Designer*
Anne Ghory-Goodman
*Photographer*
Anne Ghory-Goodman
*Agency*
GTM Design
*Client*
Johnston Paper Company

*Art Director*
Thomas Starr
*Designer*
Dan Schuman
*Artist*
John Jinks
*Agency*
Thomas Starr & Associates
*Client*
Grange Communications

*Art Director*
Anna Berkenbusch
*Designer*
Anna Berkenbusch
*Agency*
Denk Neu!
*Client*
Ottokar Runze Filmproduktion

**THE 13TH CLEVELAND INTERNATIONAL**

# FILM FESTIVAL

APRIL 4, OHIO THEATRE · APRIL 7-16, CEDAR LEE THEATRE

# FILMFEST D.C.

**FIRST ANNUAL WASHINGTON, D.C. INTERNATIONAL FILM FESTIVAL   APRIL 22-MAY 3, 1987**

*Director*
n Lionti
*signer*
n Lionti
*otographer*
orge Remington
*ency*
gett-Stashower Advertising
*nt*
veland In' ʌ. ʜlm Festival

*Art Director*
Burkey Belser
*Designers*
Tracy Keiser, Craig Byers
*Agency*
Greenfield/Belser Ltd.
*Client*
Filmfest D.C.

ETTA JENKS

**PLAYWRIGHT**
**MARLANE MEYER**
**DIRECTOR**
**M. BURKE WALKER**

AN UNFORGETTABLE TWIST ON THE RISE OF A HOPEFUL, YOUNG HOLLYWOOD STARLET

**OPENS**
**JANUARY 3, 1990**

**THE EMPTY SPACE THEATRE**
PIONEER SQUARE
107 OCCIDENTAL AVE S

**EMPTY SPACE**

**TICKETS**
**467-6000**

*Art Director*
Susan Dewey
*Designer*
Margo Sepanski
Photographer
Karen Moskowitz
*Agency*
NBBJ, Seattle
*Client*
The Empty Space Theatre

GNADENLOS
DEUTSCH

HORST SCHROTH                    ACHIM KONEJUNG

INSZENIERUNG:ULI WALLER          AUSSTATTUNG:BRITTA HANSEN

Art Director
Simone Konejung
Designer
Simone Konejung
Client
Horst Schroth/
Achim Konejung

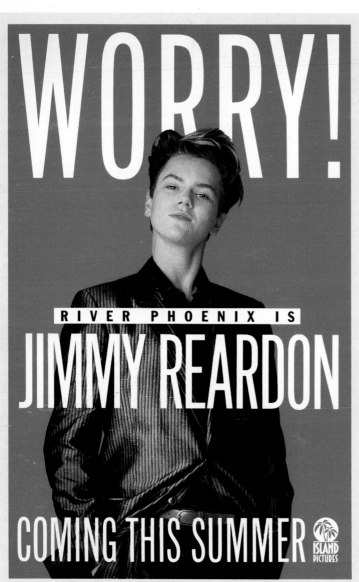

**WORRY!**

RIVER PHOENIX IS

**JIMMY REARDON**

COMING THIS SUMMER — ISLAND PICTURES

**ADRIAN**

UND DIE RÖMER

DARSTELLER
**Klaus Bueb
Gertraud Jesserer
Katharina Abt
Sabine von Maydell
Gert Haucke
Ulrich Wildgruber
Hark Bohm**
DREHBUCH
**Klaus Bueb**
KAMERA
**Thomas Mauch**
MUSIK
**Claus Bantzer**
SCHNITT
**Ursula West**
AUSSTATTUNG
**Beate Langmaack**
PRODUKTIONSLEITUNG
**Michael Beier**
PRODUKTION
**Ottokar Runze**
REGIE
**Klaus Bueb
Thomas Mauch**
VERLEIH
**Impuls Film**

*Art Director*
Lucinda Cowell
*Designer*
Michael Hodgson
*Agency*
Concept Arts
*Client*
Island Pictures

*Art Director*
Anna Berkenbusch
*Designer*
Anna Berkenbusch
*Agency*
Denk Neu! GmbH
*Client*
Impuls Film

*Art Director*
Barbara Sudick
*Designer*
Barbara Sudick
*Copywriter*
Robert Wildman
*Agency*
Nighswander Sudi
*Client*
Yale Repertory The

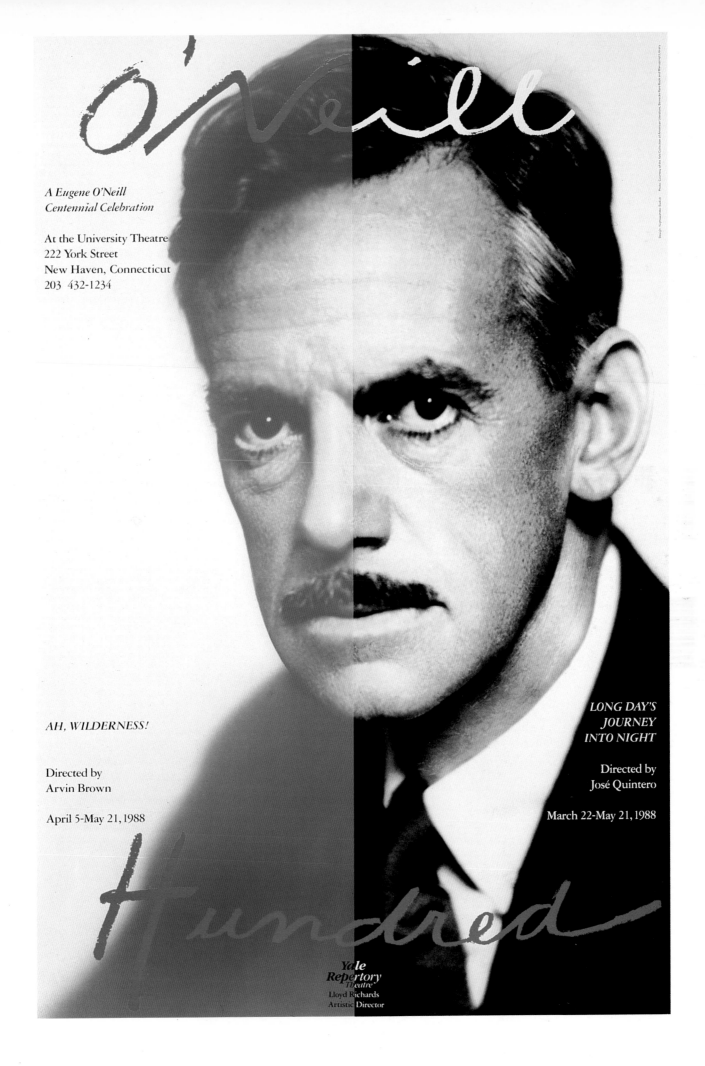

**O'Neill**

A Eugene O'Neill
Centennial Celebration

At the University Theatre
222 York Street
New Haven, Connecticut
203 432-1234

*AH, WILDERNESS!*

Directed by
Arvin Brown

April 5-May 21, 1988

*LONG DAY'S
JOURNEY
INTO NIGHT*

Directed by
José Quintero

March 22-May 21, 1988

*Hundred*

**Yale
Repertory**
*Theatre*
Lloyd Richards
Artistic Director

**LIDO CANTARUTTI PRESENTS THE 1988**

# ITaLIaN FILM FESTIVaL

**July 9 – July 30
8:00 PM
Forest Meadows,
Dominican College
and
Fine Arts Theatre,
College of Marin**

At the outdoor theatre in Forest
Meadows, Dominican College:

**Marriage Italian Style**
(Matrimonio all'italiana)
Directed by Vittorio De Sica
Starring Sophia Loren and
Marcello Mastroianni
July 9

**The Railroad Man**
(Il ferroviere)
Directed by and starring Pietro Germi
July 16

At the Fine Arts Theatre, College of Marin:

**Bread, Love and Jealousy**
(Pane, amore e gelosia)
Directed by Luigi Comencini
Starring Vittorio De Sica and
Gina Lollobrigida
July 23

**Three Brothers**
(Tre fratelli)
Directed by Francesco Rosi
Starring Vittorio Mezzogiorno,
Phillippe Noiret, Michele Placido
and Charles Vanel
July 30

Presented by Lido Cantarutti, in
co-production with Dominican College
and Marin Community Playhouse
and co-sponsorship with the Marin
Community College.

Tickets available for purchase through
the box offices for Forest Meadows,
415 457-0811, or for the College of Marin,
415 485-9385.

Design: Michael Osborne Design, Inc.
Typography: Andresen Typographics of San Francisco
Printing: Seripheus/David Smith

*Art Director*
Michael Osborne
*Designers*
Michael Osborne,
Elizabeth Burrill
*Agency*
Michael Osborne Design
*Client*
Lido Cantarutti

*Creative Director*
Ruedi Wyler
*Art Director*
Markus Cavegn
*Photographer*
Julien Vonier
*Agency*
Ruedi Wyler Werbung
*Client*
Präsidialabteilung der
Stadt Zürich

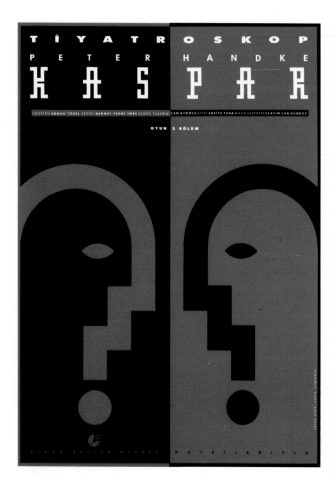

Art Directors
Savas Cekic, Sahin Aymergen
Designers
Savas Cekic, Sahin Aymergen
Agency
Valör Design Promotion Agency
Client
Goethe Institut

Designer
Eugen Bachmann-Geiser
Illustrator
Johannes Grützke
Client
Neue Schauspiel AG

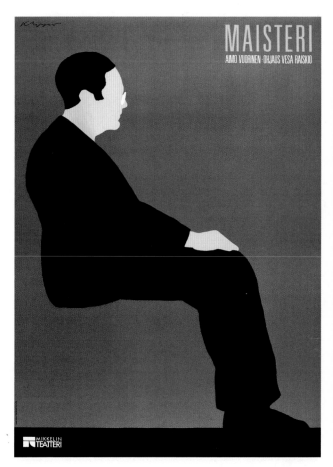

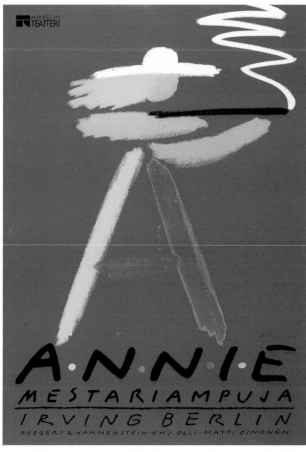

Art Director
Kari Piippo
Designer
Kari Piippo
Agency
Kari Piippo Oy
Client
Mikkelin Teatteri

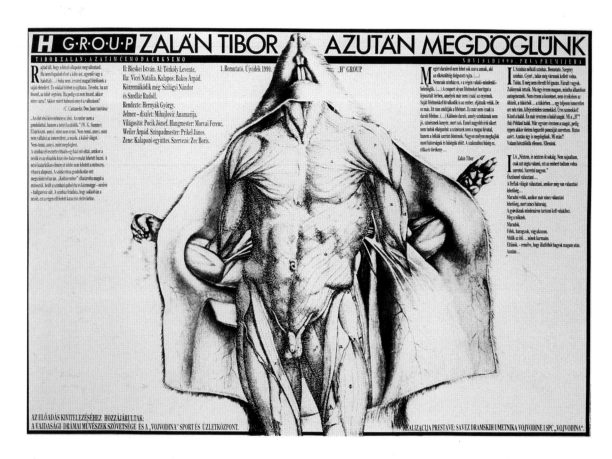

*Art Director*
Ferenc Barat
*Designer*
Ferenc Barat
*Client*
H-Group

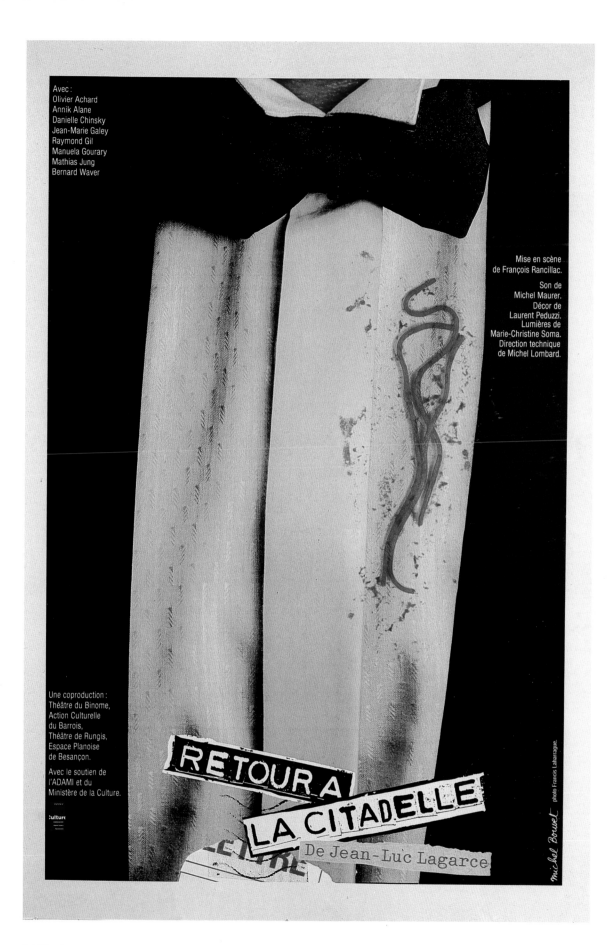

Art Director
Michel Bouvet
*Designer*
Michel Bouvet
*Photographer*
Francis Laharrague
*Client*
Theatre du Binome

Art Directors
Gabi Koloss-Müller,
Karl Müller
Designers
Gabi Koloss-Müller,
Karl Müller
Photographers
Gabi Koloss-Müller,
Karl Müller
Agency
Moderne Reklame
Client
Evangelische Erwachse-
nenbildung Frankfurt

Art Director
Joze Domjan
Designer
Joze Domjan
Illustrator
Joze Domjan
Agency
Galeria Izba
Client
Theater Celje

# PAT, *een koningsspel*

Vrij van zegel - Printed in Belgium by Printo - Aartselaar 03/8872021

## Nieuw Ensemble RaamTeater

Van Pavel Kohout / VERTALING: JAN CHRISTIAENS / REGIE: WALTER TILLEMANS
DECOR: MARC CNOPS / KOSTUUMS: ERNA SIEBENS
MET LUC PHILIPS, BERT ANDRE EN JULIENNE DE BRUYN

### 't klein Raamteater
Lange Gasthuisstr. 26
**Van 12 Mei t/m 25 Juni**
Op Wo., Do., Vr. en Za. om 20.00u. En Zo. om 15.00u.
Reservatie: 03/2339148/49

*Director*
*arcin Mroszczak*
*signer*
*arcin Mroszczak*
*otographer*
*arles Joux*
*ency*
*rporate Images*
*ent*
*am Theater, Antwerpen*

American Conservatory Theater 1990 Summer Training Congress

Art Director
Steven Tolleson
Designers
Renée Sullivan,
Steven Tolleson
Photographer
Luis Delgado
Agency
Tolleson Design
Client
American Conservatory
Theater

Art Director
Penny Howarth
Designer
Penny Howarth
Studio
Rod Dyer Group Inc.
Client
Vestron Pictures

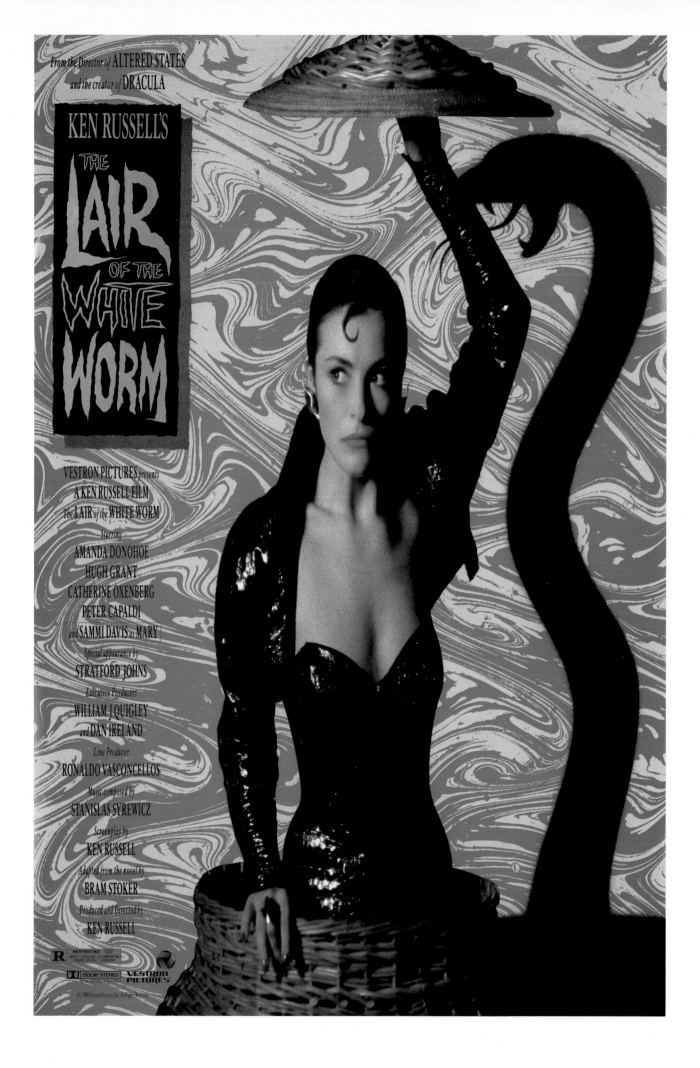

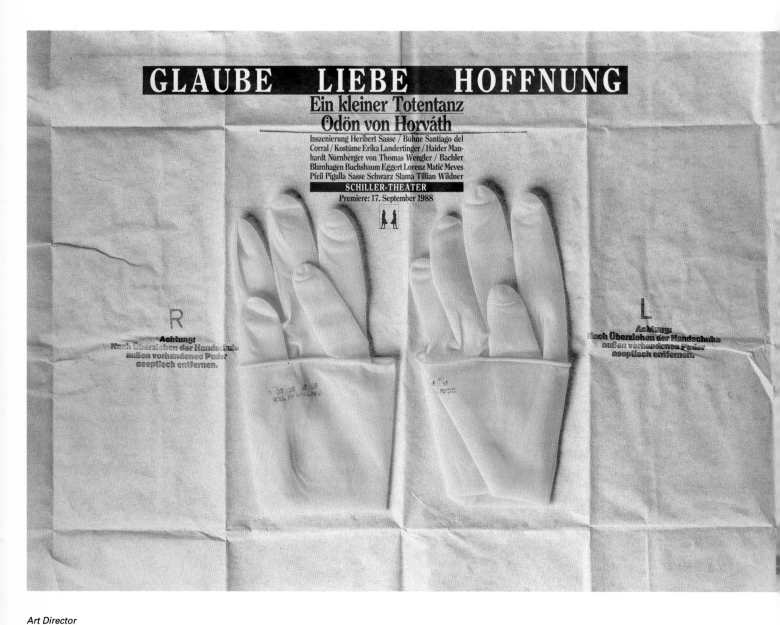

Art Director
Holger Matthies
Designer
Holger Matthies
Artist
Holger Matthies
Client
Schiller-Theater, Berlin

Art Director
Koichi Sato
Designer
Koichi Sato
Agency
Koichi Sato Design Stu
Client
Ongakuza Company

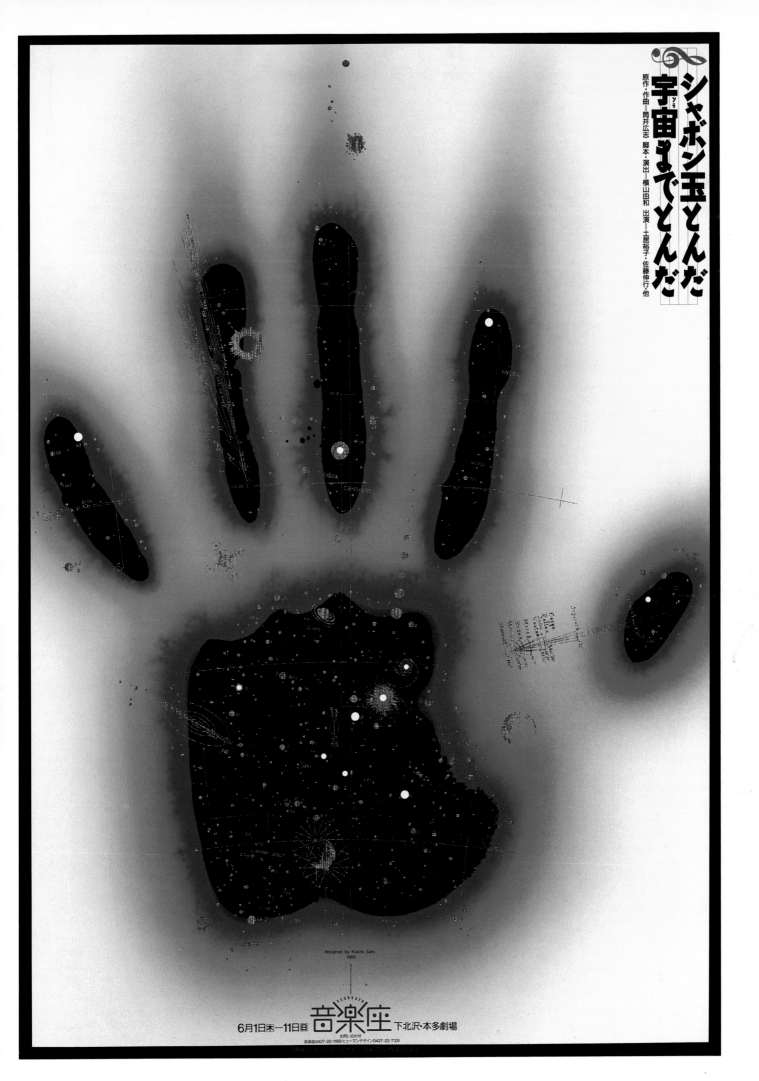

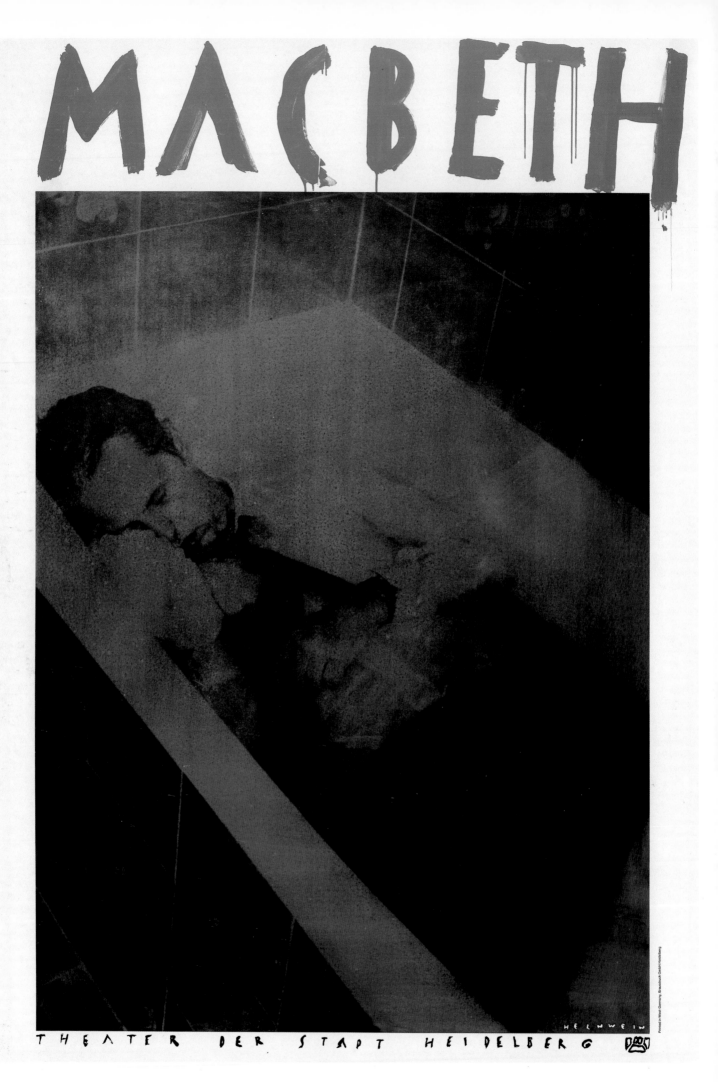

*Director*
tfried Helnwein
*signer*
tfried Helnwein
*ist*
tfried Helnwein
*ent*
eater Heidelberg

**THE CLASSIC GANGSTER TALE**
Opens June 20th
at the
**Organic Theater Company**
3319 N. Clark St., Chicago
Tickets: 327 5588

Novel by W.R. Burnett
Adapted by Michael Miner & Thomas Riccio
Directed by Thomas Riccio
Music Composed by Charles Wilding-White
Set Design by Greg Mowery
Light Design by James Card
Costume Design by Malgorzata Komorowksa
Prop Design by Brendon deVallance
Multimedia by Mark McKernin
Poster design by Art Chantry (Seattle)

*Director*
Chantry
*signer*
Chantry
*ncy*
Chantry Design
*nt*
Organic Theater
mpany, Chicago

## Fast 400 Jahre Hamlet, und Sie kennen immer noch nur dieses eine Zitat?

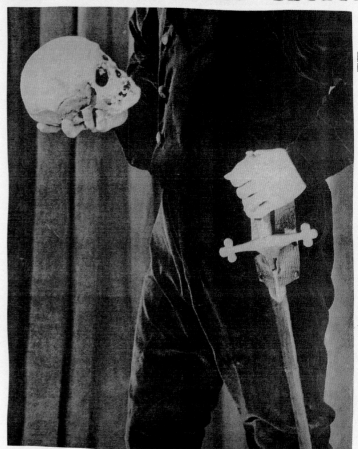

HAMLET von William Shakespeare. Premiere am 28.10.88. Der neue Schauspieldirektor und das neue Ensemble laden Sie herzlich zur neuen Spielzeit 1988/89 ein. Weitere Premieren: Peer Gynt am 14.9.88. QUAI WEST am 23.9.88. ICH BIN NICHT RAPPAPORT am 30.9.88. REPORTER am 26.11.88. Und weitere Produktionen im Kleinen Haus, im Kammertheater und im neuen Theater im Depot.

schau spiel

*Art Director*
Helmut Rottke
*Designers*
Nina Ahlers,
Ulrike Kleine
*Photographers*
Hans-Jörg Michel,
Sinje Dillenkofer
*Copywriter*
Reinhold Scheer
*Agency*
Rottke Werbung
*Client*
Staatstheater Stuttgart

*Art Director*
Holger Matthies
*Designer*
Holger Matthies
*Artist*
Holger Matthies
*Client*
Saarländisches Staatstheater

1
*Designer*
Raphie Etgar
*Client*
The Khan Theatre

2
*Art Director*
Peter Good
*Designer*
Peter Good
*Illustrator*
Peter Good
*Photographer*
Jim Coon
*Copywriter*
Steve Campo
*Agency*
Peter Good Graphic Design
*Client*
Theaterworks

3
*Art Director*
Esmail Shishehgaran
*Designer*
Esmail Shishehgaran
*Illustrator*
Esmail Shishehgaran
*Copywriter*
Esmail Shishehgaran
*Agency*
Esmail Shishehgaran
*Client*
Esmail Shishehgaran

4, 6
*Art Director*
Sabine Kranz
*Illustrator*
Sabine Kranz
*Client*
Gesamthochschule Kassel

5, 7, 9
*Art Director*
Ferenc Barat
*Designer*
Ferenc Barat
*Illustrator*
Ferenc Barat
*Stylist*
Ferenc Barat
*Photographer*
Laszlo Dorman
*Client*
Novosadsko Pozoriste

8
*Art Director*
Jiri Janda
*Designer*
Jiri Janda
*Illustrator*
Jiri Janda
*Agency*
Jiri Janda

*Art Director*
Günther Kieser
*Designer*
Günther Kieser
*Artist*
Günther Kieser
*Agency*
Hessischer Rundfunk/
Abt. Publizistik
*Client*
Hessischer Rundfunk

▷ *Art Director*
Jean-Marc Barrier
*Designer*
Jean-Marc Barrier
*Photographer*
AVEC
*Agency*
Jean-Marc Barrier
*Client*
Bibliothèque Municipale
d'Annecy

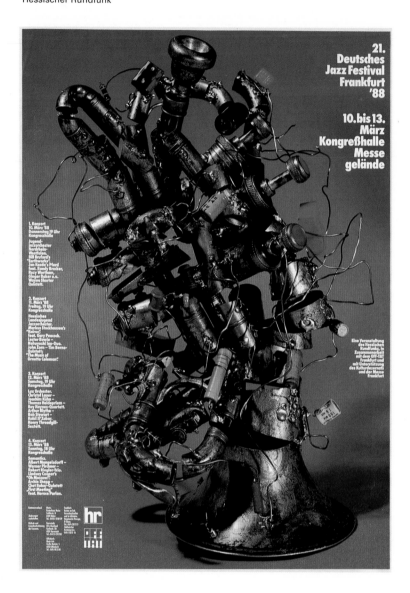

▷▷ *Art Director*
Niklaus Troxler
*Designer*
Niklaus Troxler
*Artist*
Niklaus Troxler
*Copywriter*
Niklaus Troxler
*Agency*
Grafik-Studio Niklaus Troxler
*Client*
Jazz in der Aula, Baden

▷▷▷ *Art Director*
Milton Glaser
*Designer*
Milton Glaser
*Artist*
Milton Glaser
*Agency*
Milton Glaser, Inc.
*Client*
Queens College of the City
University of New York

# Espace Musical Jan.89|Avr.89

espace musical
le vendredi
à 18 heures
espace 60
bonlieu annecy
entrée libre
renseignements
50 45 78 98

vendredi
13 janvier
chansons
de la mer
et de l'eau
hai collomb
patrick mathis

vendredi
20 janvier
claudio
monteverdi
renée petinot

vendredi
3 février
musique et sport
une expérience
électro-
acoustique
marie-noëlle ramuz
ph. moënne-loccoz

vendredi
24 février
musiques
de grèce
ensemble
skaros

vendredi
3 mars
f... comme
fête à la
francophonie
europ'arts
trio
alain carré
g. gogniat
p. nazarian

vendredi
17 mars
tout va
très bien
madame
la marquise
jean-claude
pierre

vendredi
14 avril
rimbaud
alain carré
jacky détraz

vendredi
21 avril
silences,
soupirs et
différences
handicap et
musique...
présenté par
alain goudard

addim 74
La Bibliothèque

# Espace Musical Oct.88|Déc.88

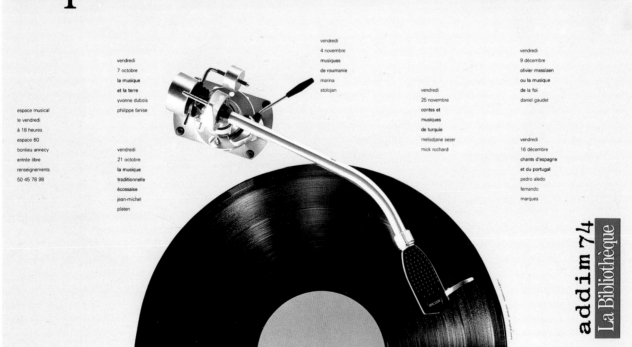

espace musical
le vendredi
à 18 heures
espace 60
bonlieu annecy
entrée libre
renseignements
50 45 78 98

vendredi
7 octobre
la musique
et la terre
yvonne dubois
philippe fanise

vendredi
21 octobre
la musique
traditionnelle
écossaise
jean-michel
platen

vendredi
4 novembre
musiques
de roumanie
marina
stolojan

vendredi
25 novembre
contes et
musiques
de turquie
melisdjane sezer
mick rochard

vendredi
9 décembre
olivier messiaen
ou la musique
de la foi
daniel gaudet

vendredi
16 décembre
chants d'espagne
et du portugal
pedro aledo
fernando
marques

addim 74
La Bibliothèque

Kurtheater Baden Sonntag 22. Nov. 87, 19.00 Uhr

# TRIBUTE TO FATS WALLER

Ralph Sutton, Jim Galloway, Milt Hinton, Gus Johnson
Henri Chaix, Alain DuBois, Romano Cavicchiolo
Vorverkauf: SKA, Badstrasse 8, Baden. Tel. 056-20 12 01

FOR THE LOVE OF LOUIS. CARNEGIE HALL JUNE 24, 1988. A JAZZ SPECTACULAR.

GUEST HOST:
WHOOPI GOLDBERG

LIONEL HAMPTON
DIZZY GILLESPIE
WYNTON MARSALIS
CLARK TERRY
JIMMY OWENS
ROY ELDRIDGE
JON FADDIS
MILT HINTON
CARRIE SMITH
DICK HYMAN
JOE NEWMAN
RANDY SANDKE
RUBY BRAFF
WARREN VACHÉ, JR.
NORRIS TURNEY
HAYWOOD HENRY
JIMMY HEATH
PHIL BODNER
KENNY DAVERN
DAN BARRETT
GEORGE MASSO
EDDIE BERT
OLIVER JACKSON
HOWARD ALDEN
MARTY NAPOLEON
ARVELL SHAW

20th Annual San Luis Obispo Mozart Festival

George Stewart: Historical Figure
Scott Loy: Photography
Pierre Rademaker Design: Poster Design

*Art Director*
Pierre Rademaker
*Designer*s
Leslie McDougall,
Pierre Rademaker
*Photographer*
Scott Loy
*Model Maker*
George Stuart
*Agency*
Pierre Rademaker Design
*Client*
Martha Hand

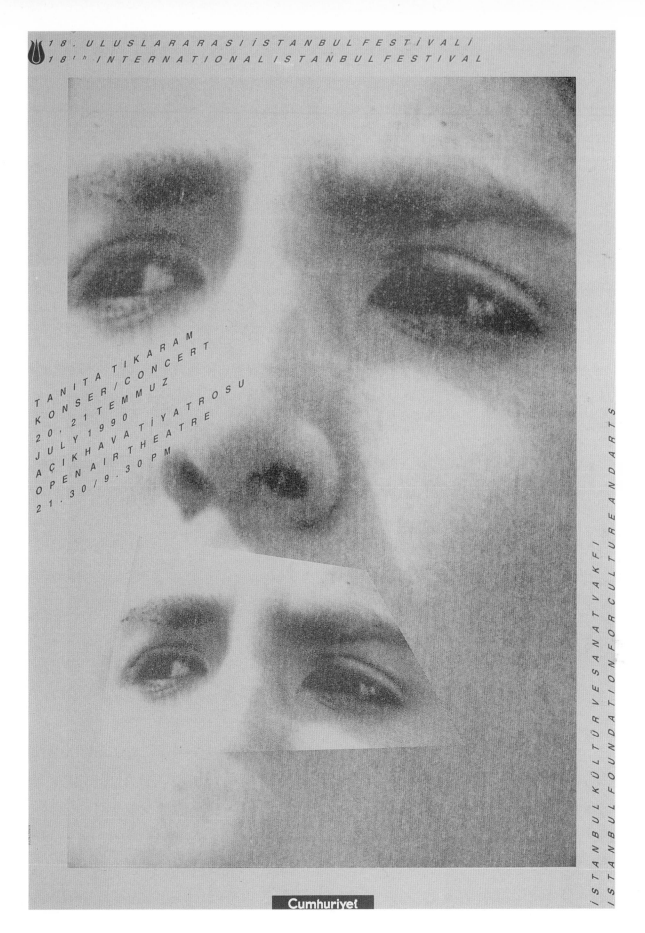

TANITA TIKARAM
KONSER/CONCERT
20, 21 TEMMUZ
JULY 1990
AÇIKHAVA TİYATROSU
OPEN AIR THEATRE
21.30/9.30 PM

İSTANBUL KÜLTÜR VE SANAT VAKFI
ISTANBUL FOUNDATION FOR CULTURE AND ARTS

Cumhuriyet

*Art Director*
Bülent Erkmen
*Designer*
Bülent Erkmen
*Illustrator*
Bülent Erkmen
*Agency*
Reklamevi Y&R
*Client*
Cumhuriyet Daily

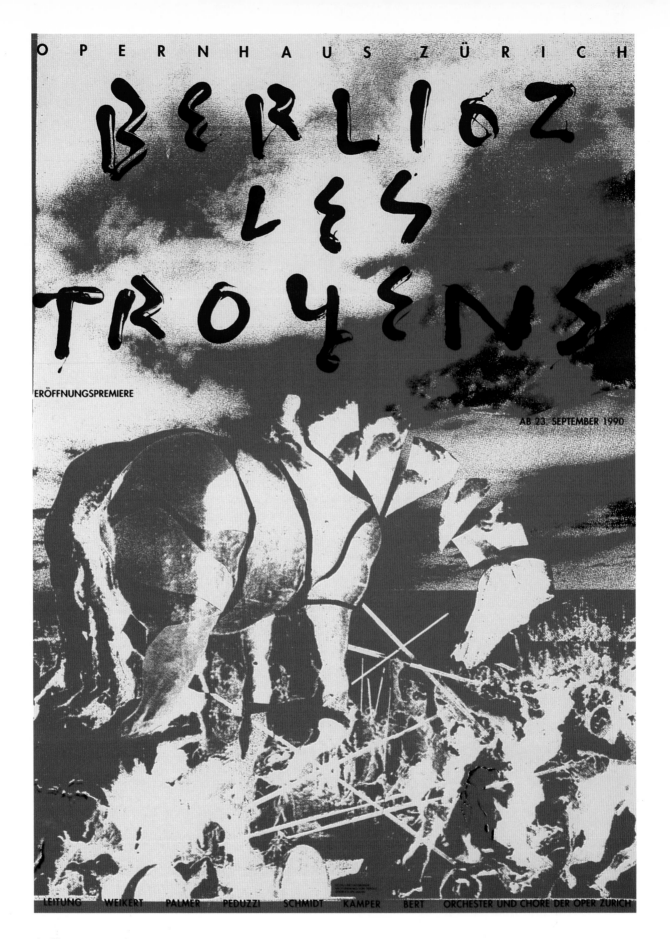

Art Director
K. Domenic Geissbühler
Designer
K. Domenic Geissbühler
Illustrator
K. Domenic Geissbühler
Agency
K. Domenic Geissbühler
Client
Opernhaus Zürich

Art Director
Ferenc Barat
Designer
Ferenc Barat
Illustrator
Ferenc Barat
Client
Zvezdara Teatar

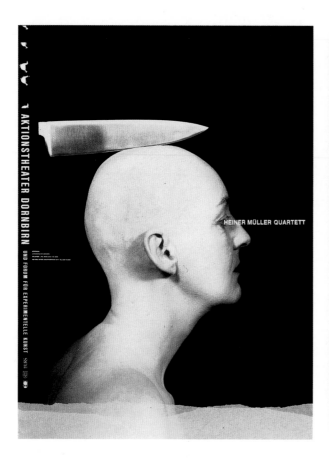

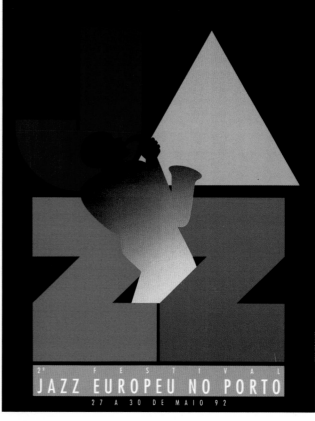

Art Director
Sigi Ramoser
Designer
Sigi Ramoser
Photographer
Herbert Neuner
Agency
Sigi Ramoser
Client
Aktionstheater Dornbirn

Art Director
Joao Machado
Designer
Joao Machado
Illustrator
Joao Machado
Client
Camara Municipal
do Porto

*Art Director*
Niklaus Troxler
*Designer*
Niklaus Troxler
*Illustrator*
Niklaus Troxler
*Agency*
Grafik-Studio
Niklaus Troxler
*Client*
Jazz in Willisau

Join us for cocktails, good food and dancing to the sounds of Duck Soup.
At the Dell Computer Corporation Christmas party.
Saturday, December 17, 1988. From 8:00 until midnight. The Frank Erwin Center.

*Art Director*
Yvonne Tocquigny
*Designers*
Yvonne Tocquigny,
Pam Fisher
*Artist*
José Ortega
*Copywriter*
Mary Luschin
*Agency*
Tocquigny Design, Inc.
*Client*
Dell Computer Corporation

In concert.

Zack Burris Photography Inc. Chicago

*Designer*
Zack Burris
*Photographer*
Zack Burris
*Client*
Yamaha Corp.

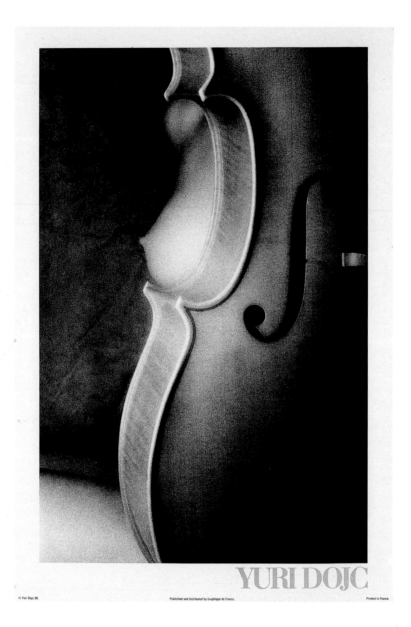

Designer
Studio Innova
*Photographer*
Yuri Dojc
*Publisher*
Graphique de France

SILHOUETTES · DARRELL PETERSON

*Art Directors*
rrell Peterson,
lliam Allen
*signer*
lliam Allen
*otographer*
rrell Peterson
*ency*
lliam Allen & Assoc.
*blisher*
eanic Poster Co.

Art Director
John Constable
Designer
John Constable
Photographer
David VanderVeen
Copywriter
Kirk Ruhnke
Agency
Frankenberry, Laughlin
& Constable
Client
David VanderVeen
Photography

# WHO'S AFRAID OF THE BIG IDEA, THE BIG IDEA.

An editorial comment from Biff, Bait, Hack, & Barryl.

Director
Mayer
signer
Anwyl
st
Mayer
ywriter
Richardson
nt
Mayer

Just what L.A. needs. Another photographer.

*David Kramer is new in town and represented by Debbie Tos. (213) 466-0033.*

*Art Director*
John Vitro
*Photographer*
David Kramer
*Copywriter*
John Robertson
*Agency*
Vitro Robertson
*Client*
David Kramer
Photography

*Art Director*
Steve Sweitzer
*Photographer*
Ben Saltzman
*Copywriter*
Jarl Olsen
*Agency*
Fallon McElligott
*Client*
Ben Saltzman

NINAONA
JOTO

*Art Director*
Joel Fuller
*Designer*
Mark Cantor
*Photographer*
Nick Norwood
*Agency*
Pinkhaus Design Corp.
*Client*
Nick Norwood
Photography

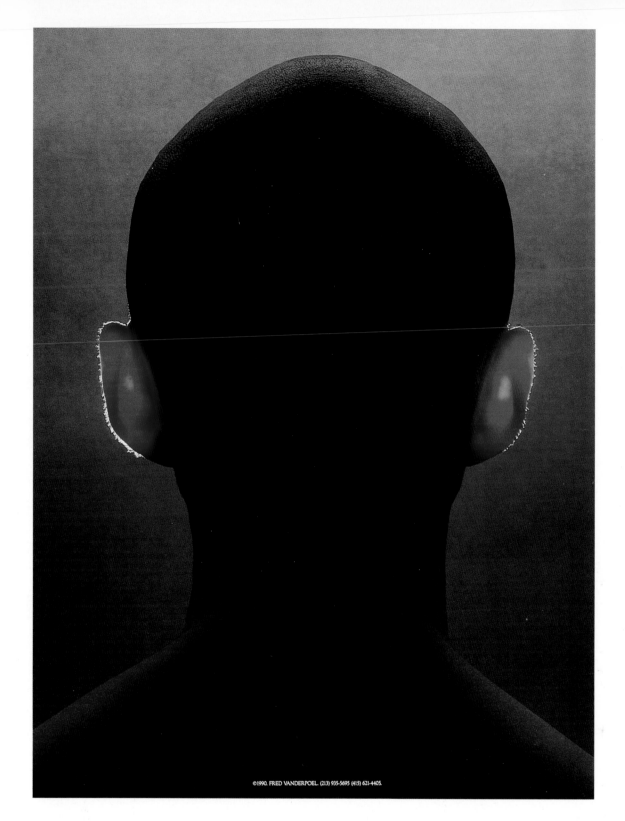

©1990. FRED VANDERPOEL. (213) 935-5695 (415) 621-4405.

*Art Director*
Tom Roth
*Photographer*
Fred Vanderpoel
*Copywriter*
Christopher Woodby
*Agency*
Anderson & Lembke
*Client*
Fred Vanderpoel
Productions

# Who's the hottest young advertising agency west of the Mississippi?

According to Adweek's September '87 *Winners* magazine, The Hively Agency is the one. And only. To take a look at some hot stuff, call David Kuhlmann at (713) 864-0295. We think you'll be mighty impressed.

The Mississippi River near St. Louis by Arthur Meyerson

*Art Director*
Charles Hively
*Designer*
Charles Hively
*Photographer*
Arthur Meyerson
*Copywriter*
Charles Hively
*Agency*
The Hively Agency
*Client*
The Hively Agency

*Art Director*
Andy Ewan
*Designer*s
Andy Ewan, Nicola Penny,
Lynne Joddrell
*Photographer*
Nicola Penny
*Agency*
The Yellow Pencil
Company
*Client*
The Yellow Pencil
Company

Designer
Joe Perrone
Photographers
Tony Gaye, Jim Quaile
Stylist
Linda Carr
Agency
G.Q. Studios Limited
Client
Prestige Graphics Inc.

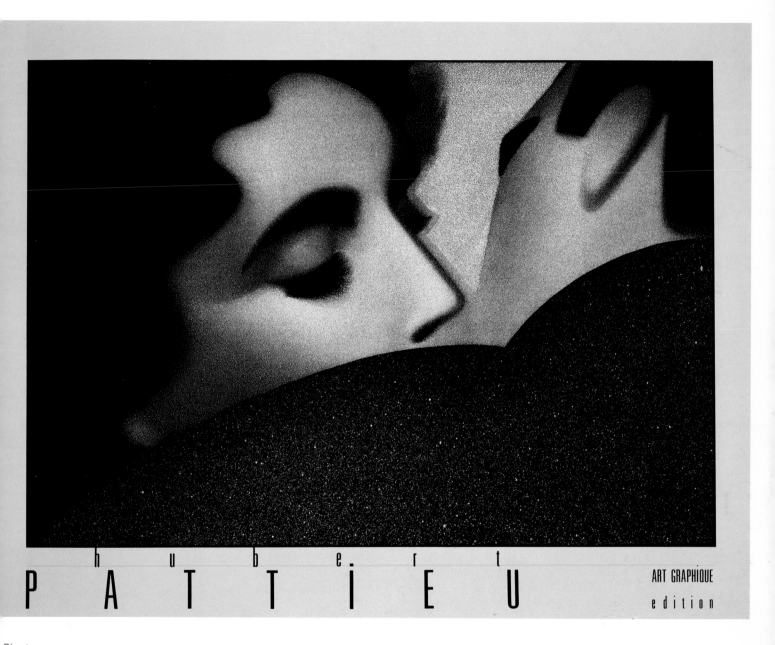

h u b e r t

# PATTIEU

**ART GRAPHIQUE**
edition

Director
ert Pattieu
signer
Benesh
st
ert Pattieu
ncy
ert Pattieu
nt
Graphique Edition

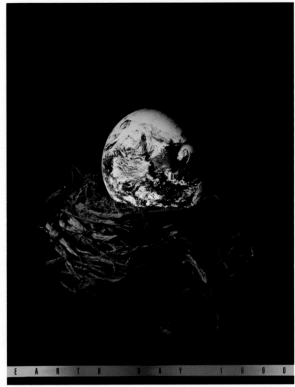

*Designer*
Michael Vanderbyl
*Agency*
Vanderbyl Design
*Client*
Exhibitor Magazine

*Art Director*
Julius Friedman
*Designer*
Julius Friedman
*Photographer*
Joyce Goldsmith
*Agency*
Images
*Client*s
Louisville Zoo,
Bernheim Foundation

*Art Director*
Terry Lesniewicz
*Designer*
Terry Lesniewicz
*Agency*
Lesniewicz Associat
*Client*
Owens-Corning
Fiberglas Corporati

EARTH DAY

We are committed to the future – and to the preservation of our planet for generations to come. We will continually work to improve how we operate our business, because we know the environment depends on all of us. Join us in accepting the responsibility and renewing our commitment.

Our products help protect our environment and conserve our precious natural resources. Our insulation conserves energy, our storage tanks protect our ground water, lighter weight glass fiber components help reduce automobile fuel consumption.

Designed By Lesniewicz Associates Inc.

**FIBERGLAS** Owens-Corning Fiberglas Corporation

*Art Director*
Takashi Akayama
*Designer*
Takashi Akayama
*Illustrator*
Takashi Akayama
*Agency*
Takashi Alayama Studio
*Client*
Takashi Alayama Studio

*Art Director*
Doug Akagi
*Designers*
Doug Akagi,
Kimberly Lentz-Powell
*Illustrator*
Hiroshi Akagi
*Agency*
Akagi Design
*Client*
Aiga San Francisco

*Art Director*
Kenichi Samura
*Photographers*
Yuriko Takagi,
Atsushi Kitagawara
*Copywriter*
Yuriko Takagi
*Agency*
Number One
Design Office Inc.
*Client*
Japan Graphic
Designers Association

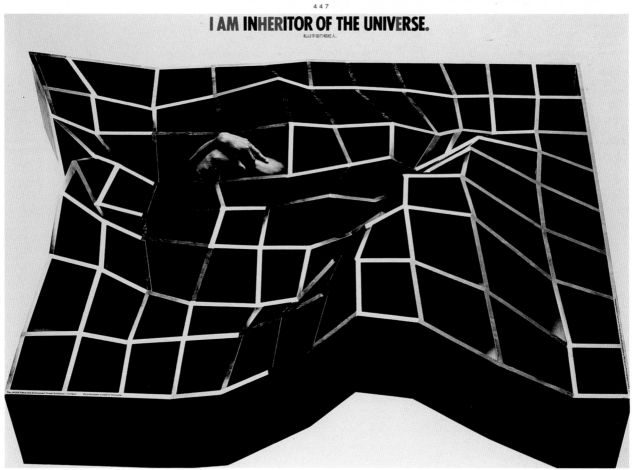

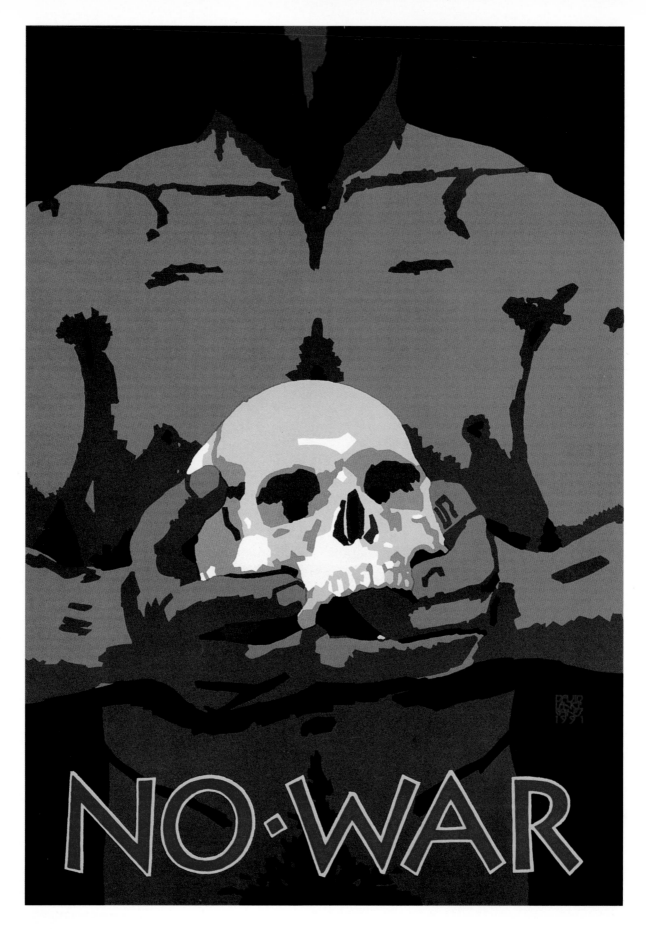

*Art Director*
David Lance Goines
*Designer*
David Lance Goines
*Illustrator*
David Lance Goines
*Agency*
Saint Hieronymus Press, Inc.
*Client*
Pro Bono Publico

*Art Director*
Keith R. Potter
*Illustrator*
Steve Lyons
*Agency*
Keith R. Potter Design
*Client*
Global Exchange

*Art Director*
Lanny Sommese
*Designer*
Lanny Sommese
*Illustrator*
Lanny Sommese
*Agency*
Sommese Design
*Client*
Sommese Design

Art Director
Ikko Tanaka
Designer
Ikko Tanaka
Artist
Ikko Tanaka
Agency
Ikko Tanaka Design Studio
Client
Hiroshima International Cultural
Foundation/Japan Graphic
Designers Association

Art Director
Takashi Fujita
Designer
Takashi Fujita
Artist
Katsumasa Tainake
Client
Japan Graphic Designers
Association

Art Director
Shin Matsunaga
Designer
Shin Matsunaga
Illustrator
Shin Matsunaga
Client
Japan Graphic Design
Association, Inc.

PEACE
*What's done cannot be undone.*
1991
Designed by Shin Matsunaga
Printed in Japan by Kyodo Printing Co.,Ltd.

*Art Director*
Shin Matsunaga
*Designer*
Shin Matsunaga
*Client*
Japan Graphic Designers
Association, Inc.

# THE TIE IS CROATIAN

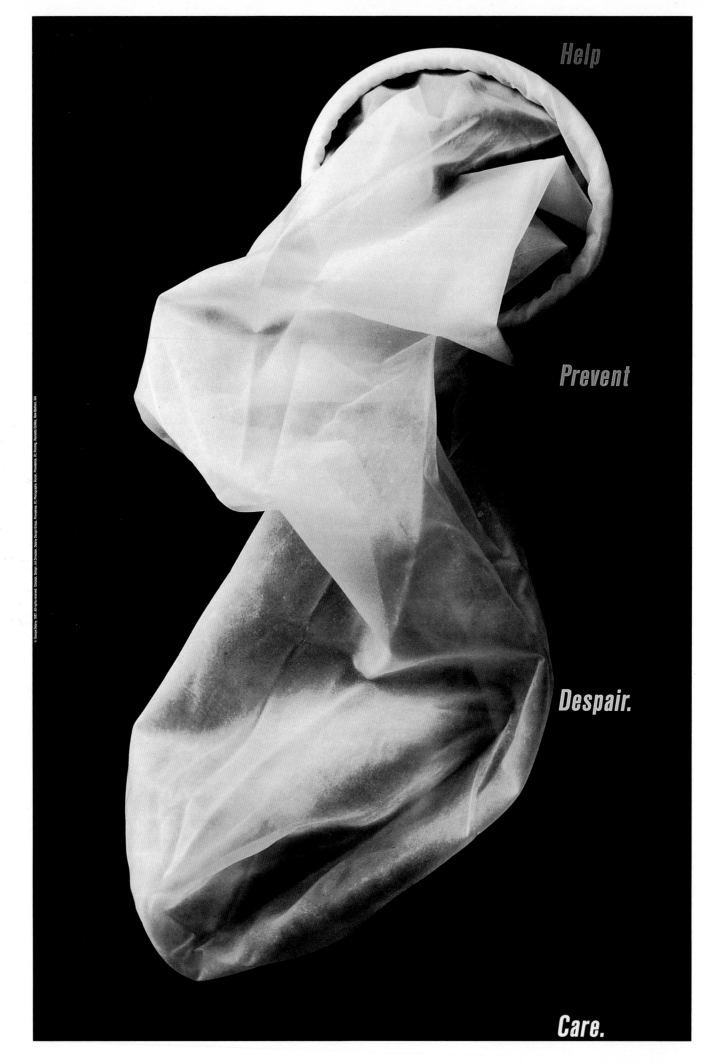

Help

Prevent

Despair.

Care.

Art Director
George Delany
Designer
George Delany
Photographer
Tyron
Copywriter
George Delany
Agency
Delany Design Group, Inc.
Client
Delany Design Group, Inc.

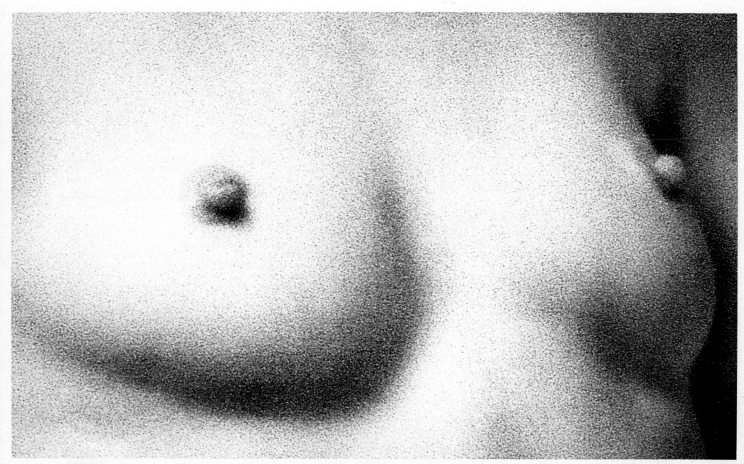

# The obscene thing is, this is a man.

Male breasts may not be the worst side effect associated with steroids — unless you're the guy playing football in a sports bra.
## STEROIDS ARE BIG TROUBLE.

Sponsored by the University of Minnesota Mens Athletic Department and "M" Club.

Art Director
Michael Fazende
Copywriter
Carl Olsen
Agency
Fallon McElligott
Client
University of Minnesota

Art Director
Boris Ljubicic
Designer
Boris Ljubicic
Illustrator
Boris Ljubicic
Copywriter
Boris Ljubicic
Stylist
Boris Ljubicic
Agency
Studio International

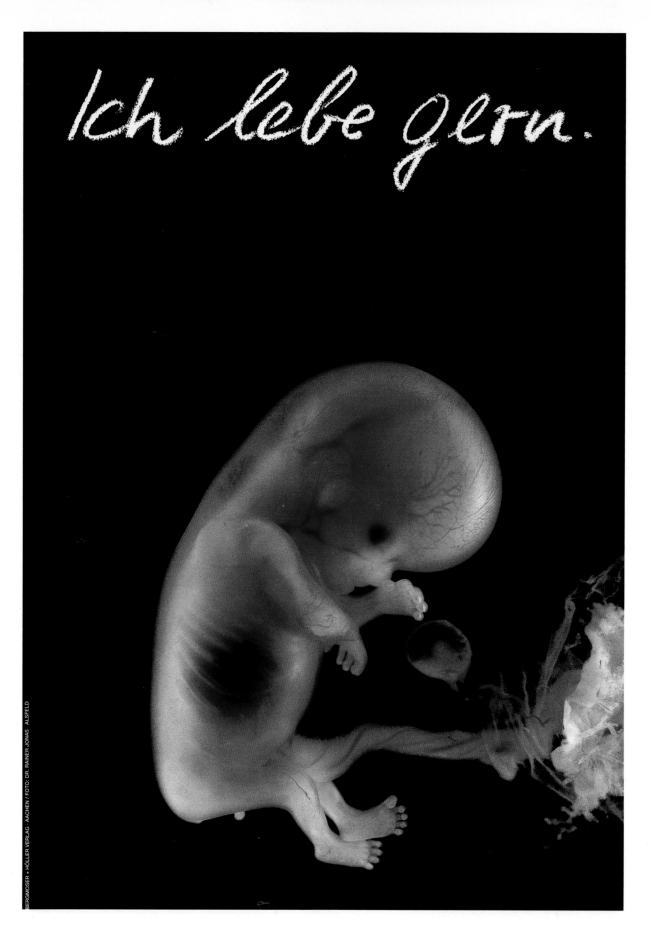

Ich lebe gern.

BERGMOSER + HÖLLER VERLAG · AACHEN / FOTO: DR. RAINER JONAS · ALSFELD

*Art Director*
Herbert Wenn
*Designer*
Herbert Wenn
*Photographer*
Rainer Jonas
*Agency*
Herbert Wenn
*Client*
Bergmoser + Höller Verlag

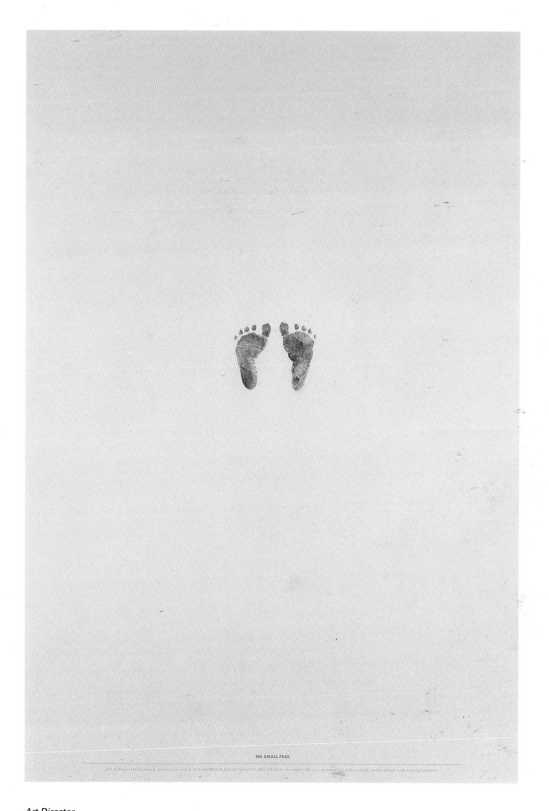

NO SMALL FEAT.

*Art Director*
Gary Templin
*Designer*
Gary Templin
*Copywriters*
Gary Templin,
Dick Mitchell
*Agency*
Richards Brock Miller
Mitchell & Assoc./
The Richards Group
*Client*
Ann & Michael McKinley

Come put on a happy face. Join Omron for lunch, New Orleans style. Which means spicy hot Cajun cooking and cool New Orleans Jazz. Make plans to be at the Commander's Palace, from 12:00 until 2:00, May 12th or 13th. It's sure to brighten your day.

*Art Director*
Jim Baldwin
*Designer*
Jim Baldwin
*Photographer*
John Wong
*Agency*
The Richards Group
*Client*
OMRON

*Art Director*
Sam Landers
*Designer*
Sam Landers
*Photographer*
Tom Maday
*Copywriters*
Gerry Weitz,
Kathy Roderick
*Agency*
Landers Larson
*Client*
Hunger Fighters
Charity Benefit

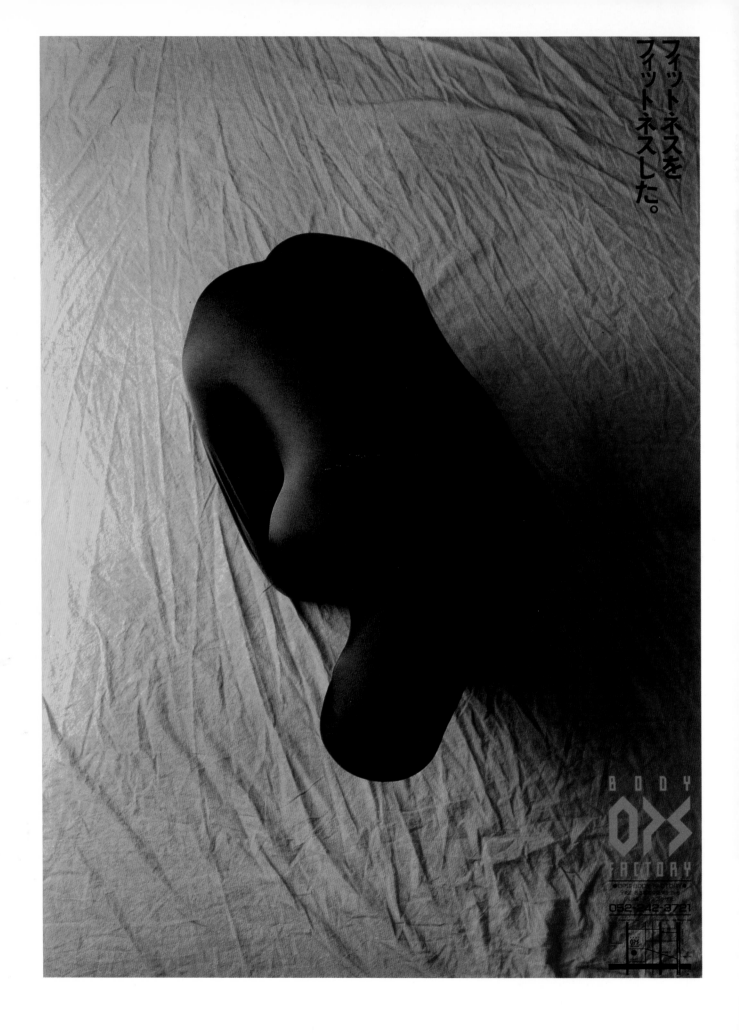

フィットネスをフィットネスした。

BODY
OX
FACTORY

t Director
asahiko Yamada
esigner
asahiko Yamada
otographer
nihiro Togawa
ylist
anami Ishikawa
opywriter
o Shinkai
gency
orkshop Yui, Inc.
ient
s Body Factory

t Director
n Dumas
signer
n Dumas
otographer
b Peterson
ency
e Design
ent
e, Inc.

Art Director
Kazuhiro Seki
Designers
Kazuhiro Seki,
Mitsue Marakami
Photographer
Sakae Takahashi
Copywriter
Toshihiro Kiuchi
Agency
Design Room AOI
Client
Hankyu Five

HANKYU **FIVE**

羽根がなくても、私は飛びます。

Art Directors
Scott Mednick,
Cheryl Rehman
Designers
Karen Chase, Loid Der
Photographer
William Hawkes
Copywriter
Peter Thornburgh
Agency
The Mednick Group
Client
Reebok International Ltd.

**APRIL 5TH THROUGH MAY 30TH** *Hooray For* HOLLYWOOD

*Art Director*
Robert Valentine
*Designer*
Robert Valentine
*Photographer*
Matthew Rolston
*Client*
Bloomingdale's

▷ *Art Director*
Makoto Saito
*Designer*
Makoto Saito
*Artist*
Makoto Saito
*Client*
Alphacubic Co., Ltd.

▷▷ *Art Director*
Tyler Smith
*Designer*
Tyler Smith
*Photographer*
George Petrakes
*Stylist*
Stephanie Karandanis
*Agency*
Tyler Smith
*Client*
Sergio Bustamante

SERGIO BUSTAMANTE · JEWELRY

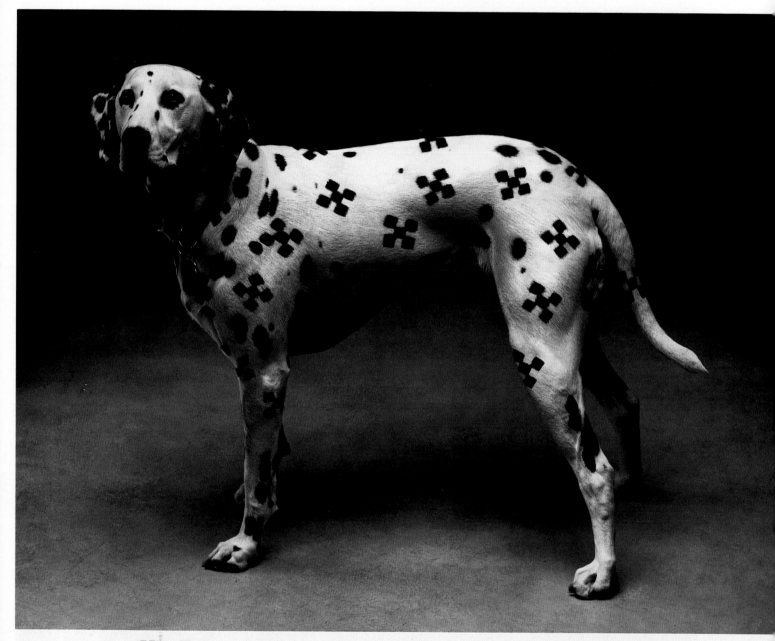

## Hire Fallon McElligott and a lot of dogs will be switching brands.
With Fallon McElligott and Ralston working together, dog owners all across the country will begin to see Purina dogfood as the only choice.

*Art Director*
Arty Tan
*Photographer*
Kerry Peterson
*Copywriter*
Mike Gibbs
*Agency*
Fallon McElligott
*Client*
Fallon McElligott

Sporting Hush Puppies.

Allow us to point out our new look. Soft leather men's casuals and women's Body Shoes—with the Comfort Curve sole to flex where your foot flexes. In a flush of spring colors.

t Director
b Barrie
otographer
ck Dublin
pywriter
rl Olsen
ency
llon McElligott
ent
sh Puppies

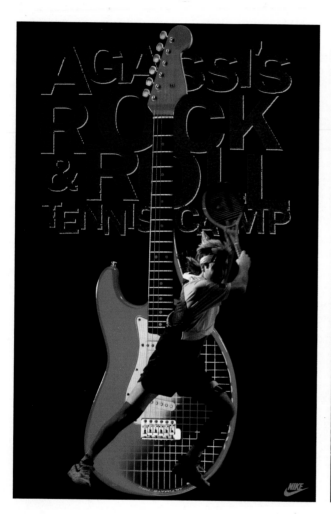

Designer
Guido Brouwers
Photographers
John Emmerling,
Pete Stone
Agency
Nike Design
Client
Nike, Inc.

Art Director
Michael Tiedy
Designer
Michael Tiedy
Photographer
Steve Dunn/
All-Sport
Illustrator
José Ortega
Agency
Nike Design
Client
Nike, Inc.

A PROCESS OF CHANGE

M A LOWER, SIMPLER

VOLUTION

FORM TO A MORE COMPLEX

OR BETTER STATE

*Art Director*
Ron Dumas
*Designer*
Ron Dumas
*Photographer*
Pete Stone, Stock
*Digital Transparency*
Raphaele Inc.
*Copywriter*
Guido Brouwers
*Agency*
Nike Design
*Client*
Nike, Inc.

▷ *Art Director*
Jeff Weithman
*Designer*
Jeff Weithman
*Photographer*
Richard Corman
*Agency*
Nike Design
*Client*s
Borussia Dortmund,
Nike, Inc.

▷▷ *Art Director*s
Charles Anderson,
Daniel Olson
*Designer*s
Charles Anderson,
Daniel Olson, Haley Johnson
*Illustrator*s
Takenobu Igarashi,
Alfons Holtgreve, Ralph Steadman,
André François, Felipe Taborda
*Agency*
C. S. Anderson Design Co.
*Client*
Wieden & Kennedy

**24 KARAT ROT.**

Kodacolor FILM Gold 200

**24 KARAT BLAU.**

Kodacolor FILM Gold 200

*Art Director*
Roland Scotoni
*Designer*
Roland Scotoni
*Photographer*
Hans Feurer
*Agency*
Young & Rubicam AG
*Client*
Kodak SA

*Art Directors*
Hiromi Inayoshi,
Miha Takagi
*Designers*
Hiromi Inayoshi,
Miha Takagi
*Photographer*
Yutaka Sakano
*Copywriter*
Aiko Hanai
*Agency*
Inayoshi Design Inc.
*Client*
Nihon Information
Center

あなたは、進化を、手にする。

N|C

Fördergemeinschaft Gutes Licht

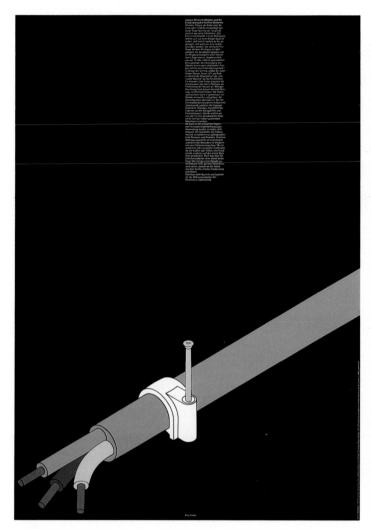

*Designer*
Alfred Kern
*Agency*
Lahaye Kern
*Client*
Kleinhuis GmbH

*Art Director*
Michael Lange
*Designer*
Michael Lange
*Photographer*
Michael Lange
*Client*
Fördergemeinschaft
Gutes Licht Darmstadt

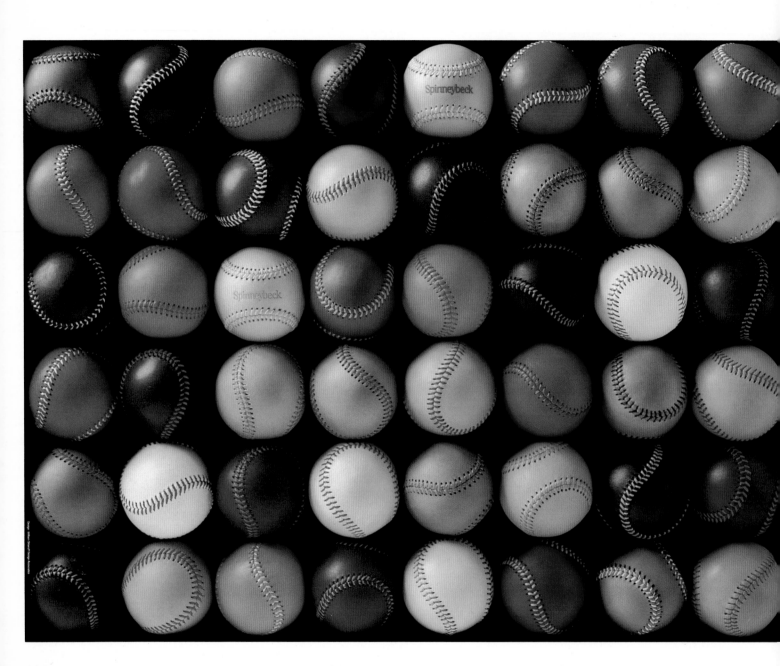

*Art Director*
William Sklaroff
*Designer*
Stephen Gray
*Photographer*
Paul Simeone
*Agency*
William Sklaroff
Design Associates
*Client*
Spinneybeck Leather

*Art Director*
Dirk Longjaloux
*Designer*
Lutz Menze
*Photographer*
Udo Kowalski
*Agency*
Hans Günter Schm
*Client*
Gira, Giersiepen
GmbH & Co KG

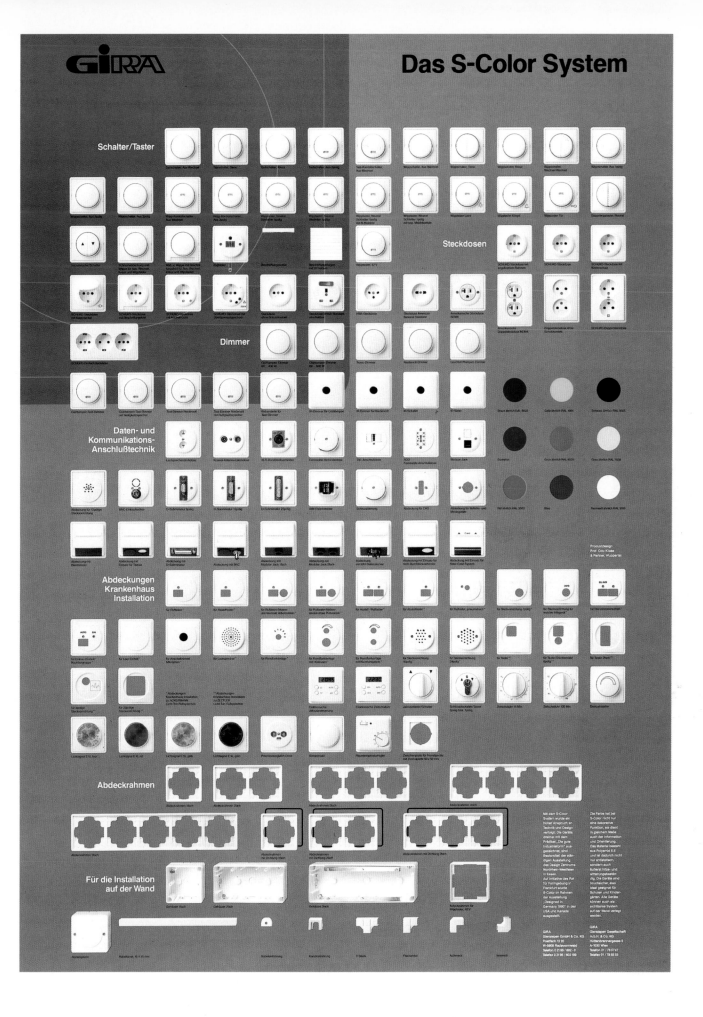

CARS
DAWYDIAK

Art Director
David Curtis
Designer
David Curtis
Illustrator
David Curtis
Agency
Curtis Design
Client
Dawydiak Cars

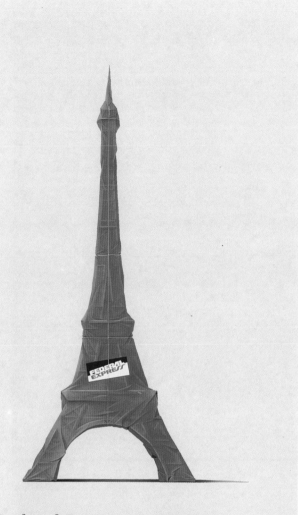

**Federal Express to France.**

**Federal Express to Germany.**

*Art Director*
Houman Pirdavari
*Designer*
Houman Pirdavari
*Artist*
Robert Giusti
*Agency*
Fallon McElligott
*Client*
Federal Express

▷ *Art Director*
John Doyle
*Designer*
John Doyle
*Photographer*
Myron
*Copywriter*
Paul Silverman
*Agency*
Mullen Adv.
*Client*
Heritage Color

▷▷ *Art Director*
Kazumasa Nagai
*Designer*
Kazumasa Nagai
*Agency*
Nippon Design Center
*Client*
Yokogawa Electric Co., Ltd.

In nature, the power of separation is basic to life. At Heritage, the power of separation is basic to life on the printed page.

Heritage Color, 222 Richmond Street, Providence, Rhode Island 02903   401-273-1500

As a company, our goal is to contribute to society through broad-ranging activities in the areas of measurement, control, and information. Individually, we aim to combine good citizenship with the courage to innovate.

YOKOGAWA

*Art Director*
Yvonne Smith
*Designer*
Yvonne Smith
*Photographer*
Lamb & Hall
*Copywriter*
Marc Descher
*Agency*
Marc Descher
& Associates
*Client*
Noritsu

*Art Director*
Tsuyoshi Fukuda
*Designer*
Hitomi Sago
*Photographer*
Katsuo Hanzawa
*Copywriter*
Yoshinari Nishimura
*Agency*
Cameleon Inc.
*Client*
NTT Nippon Telegraph &
Telephone Corp.

# CAN WE ENLARGE SOMETHING FOR YOU?
We'd be more than happy to make 5x7, 8x10 or 11x14 enlargements of your favorite prints.

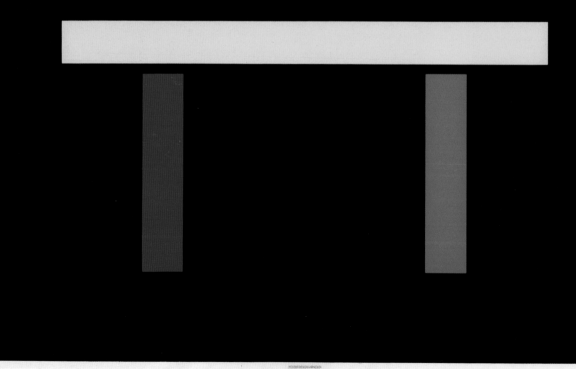

PIERRE GAGNAIRE RESTAURANT

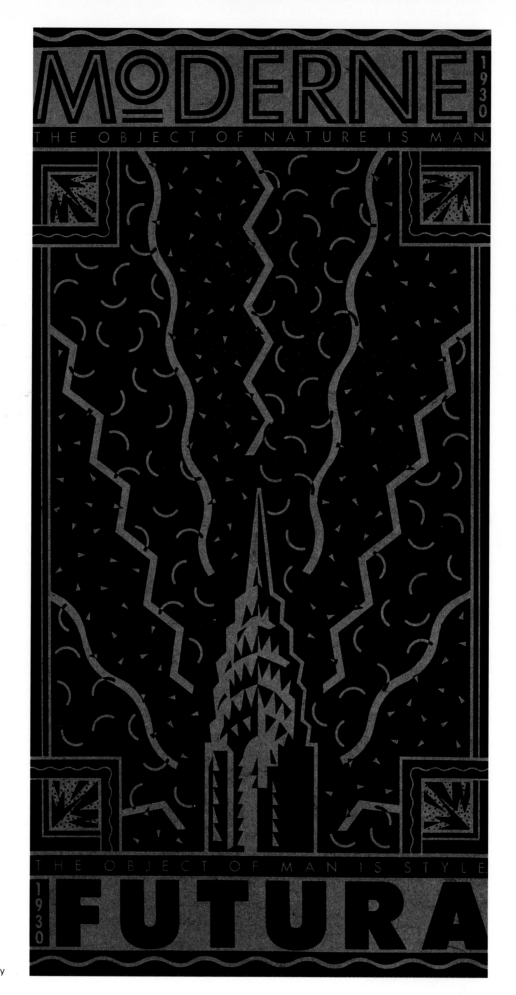

*Art Director*
Jennifer Morla
*Designer*
Jennifer Morla
*Illustrator*
Jennifer Morla
*Agency*
Morla Design
*Client*
Mercury Typography

*Art Director*
Doug Trapp
*Designer*
Doug Trapp
*Photographer*
Steve Niedorf
*Copywriter*
Jean Rhode
*Agency*
Ads Infinitum
*Client*
Letterworx Typography

▷ *Art Director*
Frank Viva
*Designer*
Frank Viva
*Illustrator*
Frank Viva
*Agency*
Frank Viva Design
*Client*
Wiggins Teape
Overseas Sales Ltd.

▷▷ *Art Director*
Michael Vanderbyl
*Designer*
Michael Vanderbyl
*Artist*
Michael Vanderbyl
*Agency*
Vanderbyl Design
*Client*
American Institute of
Architects, San Francisco

COMPETITIONS 144

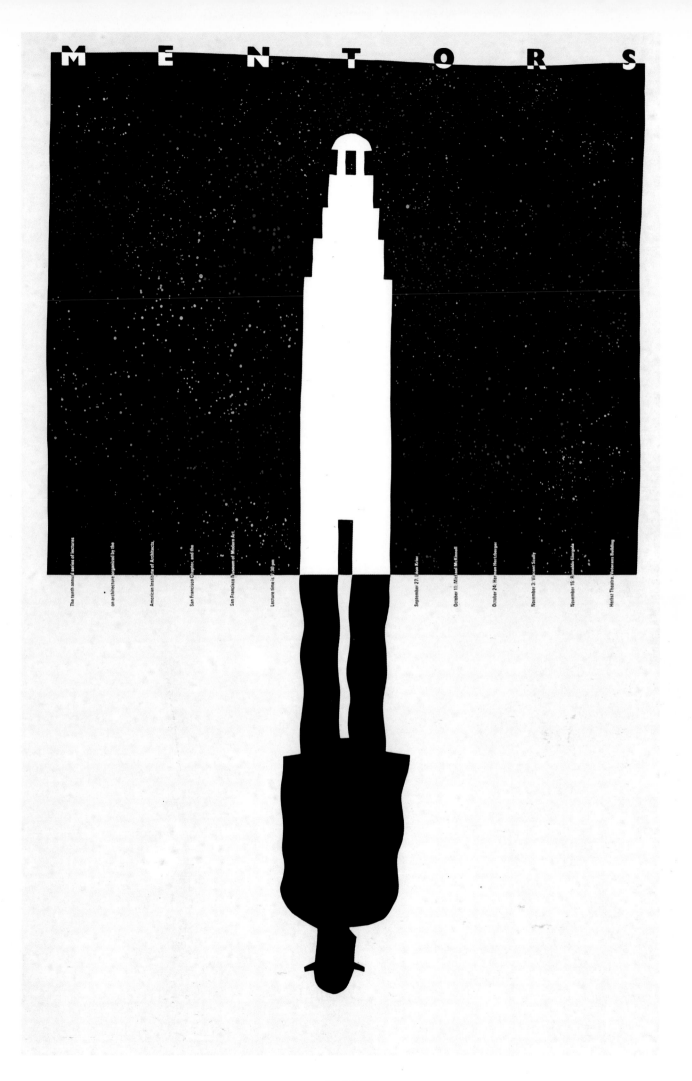

MENTORS

The tenth annual series of lectures

on architecture organized by the

American Institute of Architects,

San Francisco Chapter, and the

San Francisco Museum of Modern Art.

Lecture time is 7:30 pm

September 27: Leon Krier

October 11: Michael McKinnell

October 24: Herman Hertzberger

November 3: Vincent Scully

November 15: Romaldo Giurgola

Herbst Theatre, Veterans Building

Art Director
John Muller
Designers
Patrice Eilts, Lee Ernst,
Kent Mulkey
Photographers
Hartzell Gray (left),
David Ludwigs (right)
Copywriter
David Marks
Agency
Muller & Company
Client
Kansas City Art
Directors Club

Art Director
Michael Vande
Designer
Michael Vande
Artist
Michael Vande
Agency
Vanderbyl Des
Client
Simpson Pape
Company

**Simpson**

**Call for Entries**

The Power of the Printed Image. To astonish and delight. To be both playful and profound. To convey a message whose meaning is illuminated by form. The printed image is an idea made visible and indelible, an idea in color and form, making the connection between the eye and the mind, sight and insight, the play of the imagination and the finished work on paper.

On January 15th a distinguished jury of graphic arts professionals will celebrate the power of the printed image by selecting the winning entries in the 1987 Simpson Printed Paper Competition. This competition is held annually to recognize the skill and artistry of those who create images which compel us to stop, look, and see. Special Judges Awards and Certificates of Merit will be awarded to entries exhibiting technical and expressive achievement in design and print production on Simpson papers. Judges' Award winners will be published in *Communication Arts* Magazine. All winning entries will appear in the contest annual, as well as our traveling exhibitions.

**Jury**

Michael Vanderbyl
Vanderbyl Design
San Francisco

Nancy Skolos
Skolos, Wedell
& Raynor
Boston

John Massey
John Massey, Inc.
Chicago

**Eligibility**

Any printed piece that has been produced, in whole or in part, on any Simpson paper between January 1, 1987 and December 31, 1987 is eligible.

**Preparation of Entries**

Send three (3) samples of each entry. Attach a copy of the entry form to one of the samples. Additional entry forms are available from Simpson distributors or Simpson Paper Company. Do not mount any pieces.

**Categories**

Annual Reports

Brochures, Catalogs and Folders

Corporate Identity (Letterheads, Envelopes, Business Cards)

Books and Magazines

Posters

Other (anything not specifically covered in the above)

**Deadline**

All items must be received by Simpson no later than December 31, 1987. Any items received after that date will not be accepted for judging.

Mail Entries To
Simpson Paper Company
Awards Competition
One Post Street
San Francisco, CA
94104

Printed on
Simpson Starwhite
Vicksburg, Tiara,
Vellum, Text, 100 lb.

**Entry Form**

Title of Work

Category

Entrant's Name

Entrant's Address

Art Director/Designer

Illustrator/Photographer

Printer

Client

Paper

Paper Distributor

*Designer*
Michael Vanderbyl
*Agency*
Vanderbyl Design
*Client*
Stanford University

SAF
Syndicat des avocats
de France

La défense
au rendez-vous
européen

Droits libertés
structures

14e congrès
Colmar
12/13/14 novembre
1987

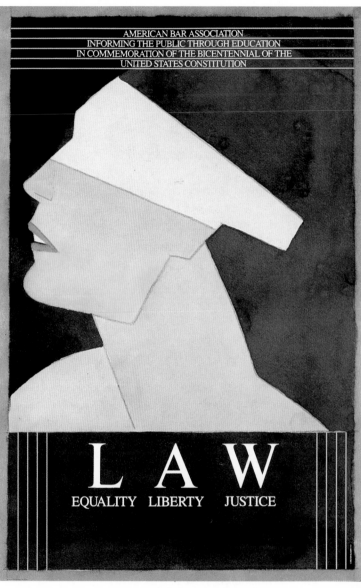

AMERICAN BAR ASSOCIATION
INFORMING THE PUBLIC THROUGH EDUCATION
IN COMMEMORATION OF THE BICENTENNIAL OF THE
UNITED STATES CONSTITUTION

# L A W
EQUALITY    LIBERTY    JUSTICE

*Director*
Gassner
*Designer*
ne Bockmühl
*ncy*
er H. P. Gassner
*nt*
Syndicat des Avocats
rance

*Art Director*
Milton Glaser
*Designer*
Milton Glaser
*Artist*
Milton Glaser
*Agency*
Milton Glaser, Inc.
*Client*
American Bar Association

Designer
Michael Vanderbyl
Agency
Vanderbyl Design
Client
San Francisco
AIA/MOMA

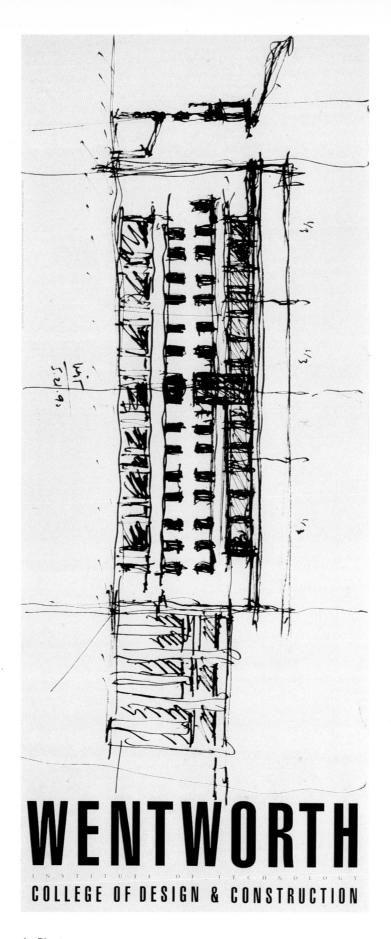

# WENTWORTH
INSTITUTE OF TECHNOLOGY
## COLLEGE OF DESIGN & CONSTRUCTION

*Art Directors*
Clifford Selbert,
Robin Perkins
*Designer*
Robin Perkins
*Illustrator*
Gabriel Yaari
*Agency*
Clifford Selbert
Design, Inc.
*Client*
Wentworth Institute
of Technology

*Art Director*
Jason Kedgley
*Designer*
Jason Kedgley
*Photographer*s
Jason Kedgley,
Carol Moss
*Copywriter*s
Jason Kedgley,
Crail Mellows,
Annmarie Kiddle
*Client*
London College
of Printing

*Designer*
Scott Ramsey
*Illustrator*
Scott Ramsey
*Agency*
Scott Ramsey Design
*Client*
Jostens Learning
Corporation

Art Director
Scotti Larson
Designer
Scotti Larson
Photographers
Kermit Hayes,
Ferderbar Studios
Copywriters
Brad Berg,
Todd Ganser
Agency
Birdsall-Voss &
Associates
Client
Racine Literacy Council

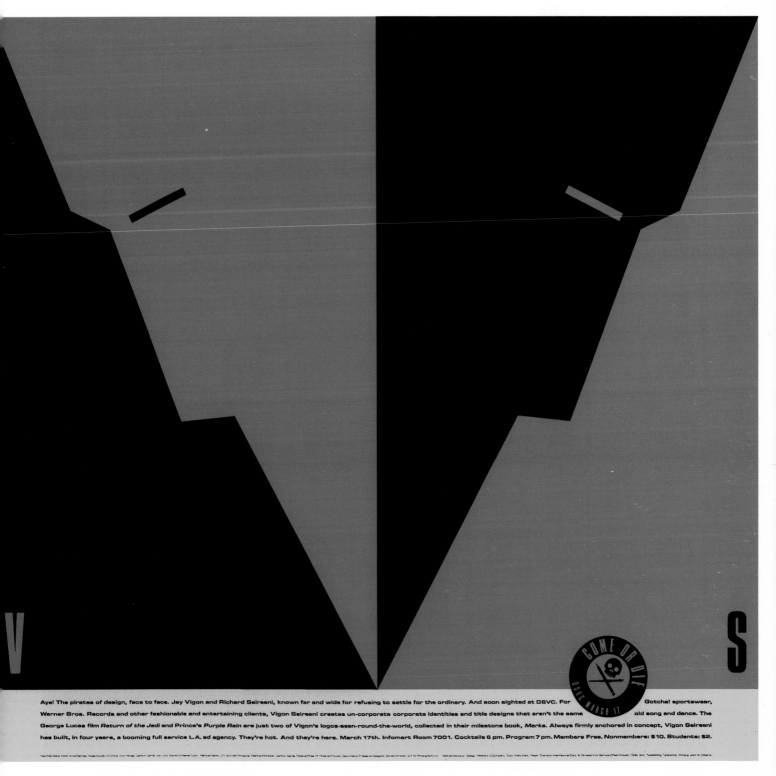

Aye! The pirates of design, face to face. Jay Vigon and Richard Seireeni, known far and wide for refusing to settle for the ordinary. And soon sighted at DSVC. For Gotcha! sportswear, Warner Bros. Records and other fashionable and entertaining clients, Vigon Seireeni creates un-corporate corporate identities and title designs that aren't the same old song and dance. The George Lucas film *Return of the Jedi* and Prince's *Purple Rain* are just two of Vigon's logos-seen-round-the-world, collected in their milestone book, *Marks.* Always firmly anchored in concept, Vigon Seireeni has built, in four years, a booming full service L.A. ad agency. They're hot. And they're here. March 17th. Infomart Room 7001. Cocktails 6 pm. Program 7 pm. Members Free. Nonmembers: $10. Students: $2.

Art Director
Scott Ray
Designer
Scott Ray
Illustrator
Scott Ray
Copywriter
Gary Keck
Agency
Peterson & Company
Client
Dallas Society of Visual
Communications

▷ Designer
Michael Bierut
*Copywriter*
Michael Bierut
*Agency*
Vignelli Associates
*Client*
New York Chapter of the
American Institute of Graphic Arts

▷▷ Art Director
Brian Boyd
*Designer*
Brian Boyd
*Artist*
Brian Boyd
*Copywriter*
Kevin Johnson
*Agency*
Richards Brock Miller
Mitchell & Assoc./
The Richards Group
*Client*
Dallas Ad League

Call for
Entries

The New York Chapter
of the American
Institute of Graphic Arts
invites all members
to submit one 35mm slide
of work of any kind
done in the past year
that represents

Your Best
Shot

The slides will be shown
at the chapter's fourth annual
opening celebration at
The Cooper-Hewitt Museum
Fifth Avenue at 91st Street
on Wednesday, September 16
from 6:30 to 8:30 pm
with food, drink and music

Entry Deadline August 31
See you there!

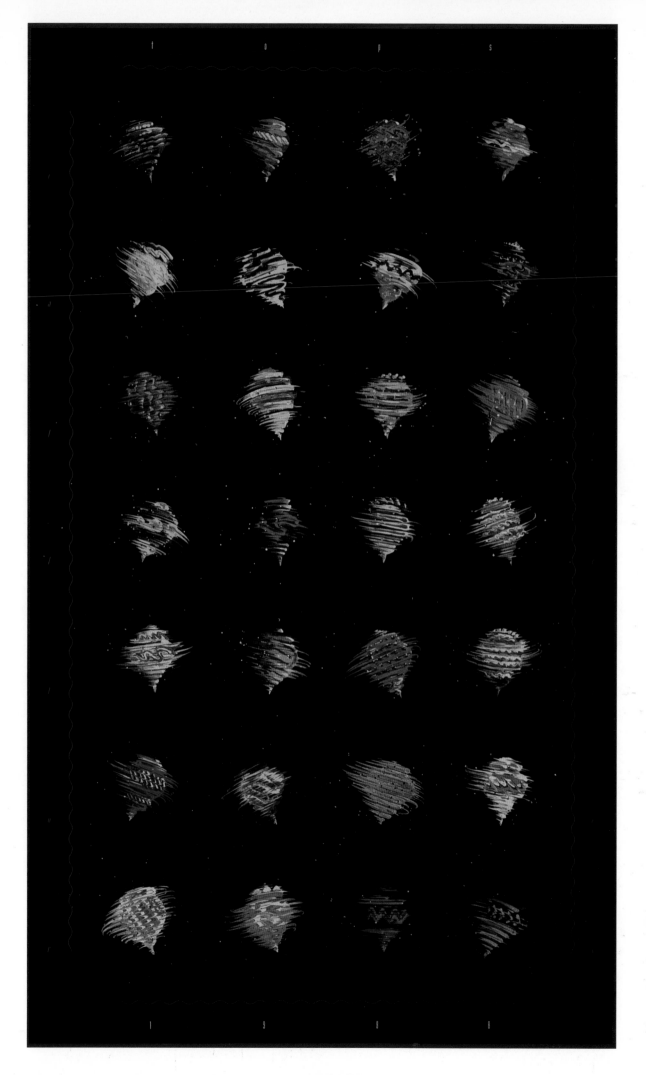

## GRAPHIS

*The International Magazine of Design and Communication*

*Die internationale Zeitschrift für Design und Kommunikation*

*Le magazine international du design et de la communication*

### Specifications:
112 Pages/Seiten

Published bi-monthly
Erscheint alle zwei Monate
Paraît tous les deux mois

Size: 9x12 inches
Format: 23x30 cm

Over 200 color plates
Über 200 Farbbilder
Plus de 200 pages en couleurs

### Contents:
The name *Graphis* carries a special meaning that for 50 years has set it apart from all other design magazines. Every other month *Graphis* brings you in-depth profiles on creative leaders in graphic design, illustration, photography, advertising, product design, and architecture and interviews with CEO's of design-directed corporations.

From cover to cover, you'll find an unmatched selection of the best creative talents each field has to offer. Since powerful visions are best evoked through powerful voices, top writers reveal the motivations and inspiration of both past masters and today's luminaries from around the world.

The leading publication of visual communication, *Graphis* is admired internationally by readers who appreciate fine design and designers who appreciate a fine read. Lavishly printed,—*Graphis* will inspire and delight you as it seeks to enlarge the quality of design on every creative front.

For information and prices in US, Canada, Asia and Pacific see the attached subscription order form or call + 1 (212) 532 9387 or fax + 1 (212) 213 3229

GRAPHIS U.S., Inc.
141 Lexington Avenue
New York, NY 10016

For information and prices in Europe, Middle East and Africa see the attached order form or call + 41 (1) 383 8211 or fax + 41 (1) 383 1643

GRAPHIS Press Corp.
Dufourstrasse 107
CH-8008 Zürich, Switzerland

### Inhalt:
*Graphis* ist seit 50 Jahren ein Begriff und hebt sich klar von anderen Design-Magazinen ab. Alle zwei Monate bringt Ihnen *Graphis* aufschlussreiche Berichte über die führenden kreativen Köpfe im Bereich des Graphik-Designs, der Illustration, der Photographie, der Werbung, der Produktgestaltung und der Architektur. Interviews mit Geschäftsführern designbewusster Unternehmen informieren über die Standpunkte der Auftraggeber.

Graphis bietet Ihnen von Ausgabe zu Ausgabe eine einmalige Auswahl der besten kreativen Leistungen in den verschiedenen Bereichen. Grosse Visionen – von grossen Stimmen kundgetan. Nur erstklassige Autoren schreiben über Motivation und Inspiration der Meister von gestern, heute und morgen – aus aller Welt. Führend im Bereich der visuellen Kommunikation, geniesst *Graphis*

international grosses Ansehen bei Lesern, die gutes Design fasziniert und bei Designern, die gute Texte schätzen. *Graphis* erscheint in allerbester Druck-qualität. Das Ziel ist, in allen Bereichen des Designs hervorragende Qualität zu fördern. Lassen Sie sich von *Graphis* inspirieren und herausfordern, und messen Sie sich und Ihre Arbeit auf internationaler Ebene.

Preisinformation für Amerika, die Pazifikländer und Asien entnehmen Sie bitte der gegenüberliegenden Bestellkarte oder über:
Tel. + 1 212 532 9387 oder
Fax + 1 212 213 3229

GRAPHIS US Inc.
141 Lexington Avenue
New York, NY 10016

Preisinformation für West- und Osteuropa, den Mittleren Osten und Afrika entnehmen Sie bitte der gegenüberliegenden Bestellkarte oder über:
Tel. + 41 1 383 82 11 oder
Fax + 41 1 383 16 43

GRAPHIS Verlag
Dufourstrasse 107
CH-8008 Zürich, Schweiz

### Sommaire:
Le nom de *Graphis* est une référence depuis 50 ans. D'emblée, ce magazine a su se distinguer des autres revues de design. Tous les deux mois, *Graphis* vous propose des reportages détaillés sur les meilleurs créatifs dans des domaines aussi variés que le design graphique, l'illustration, la photographie, la publicité, le design de produits et l'architecture. Vous y trouverez également des interviews de directeurs d'entreprises qui ont mis le design au rang de leurs priorités.

Dans chaque numéro, *Graphis* vous offre un choix unique des créations les plus remarquables réalisées dans ces divers secteurs d'activité. Des images exceptionnelles commentées par de grands noms. Vous découvrirez ainsi les motivations et les sources d'inspiration des plus grands créateurs contemporains du monde entier.

Leader dans le secteur de la communication visuelle, le magazine *Graphis* a acquis une réputation internationale auprès de lecteurs qui sont fascinés par l'esthétique du design et de profession-nels qui apprécient de bons articles.

N'hésitez plus! Abonnez-vous dès maintenant à *Graphis*. Vous pourrez y puiser à loisir idées et suggestions. Il vous permettra aussi de vous situer par rapport à la concurrence internationale.

**Vous trouverez le prix des abonnements pour l'Amérique, le Canada, l'Asie et la région du Pacifique sur la carte de commande de la page opposée. Pour plus d'information téléphonez au:**
tél. + 1 212 532 9387
fax. + 1 212 213 3229

GRAPHIS US Inc.
141 Lexington Avenue
New York, NY 10016

**Vous trouverez le prix des abonnements pour l'Europe (Est et Ouest), le Moyen-Orient et l'Afrique sur la carte de commande de la page opposée. Pour plus d'information téléphonez au:**
tél. + 41 1 383 82 11
fax. + 41 1 383 16 43

Editions GRAPHIS
Dufourstrasse 107
CH-8008 Zürich, Suisse

**BUSINESS REPLY MAIL**

FIRST CLASS PERMIT NO. 2207 NEW YORK NY

POSTAGE WILL BE PAID BY ADDRESSEE

**GRAPHIS US INC**
**141 LEXINGTON AVENUE**
**NEW YORK NY 10157-1003**

GRAPHIS PRESS CORP.
DUFOURSTRASSE 107
CH-8008 ' ZURICH
SWITZERLAND